...

twisted

night

beautiful twisted night

marc almond

●●●ellipsis

first published april 1999 by ●●●ellipsis
2 rufus street
london n1 6pe
www.ellipsis.com
...@ellipsis.co.uk

first paperback edition 1999

© marc almond 1999

drawings on pages 33, 82, 84, 87, 111
© pierre et gilles
drawing on page 20 © asako kurihara

british library cataloguing in publication
a cip record for this book is available from
the british library

isbn 1 841 66 023 x

printed in great britain
by butler & tanner, frome

●●●ellipsis is a registered trademark of
ellipsis london limited

contents

introduction

Some see the city as a cruel, dirty, heartless, selfish, soulless place and although some of this is true, I see the city as a beautiful romantic place – a playground of fantasy and desire. An amorphous beautiful monster pulsing with heart and soul. A complicated network of lives – some on a solitary path but many interchanging, passing in a moment, loving, working, and sometimes killing. Life on different levels. A visible world on view, seemingly respectable, simple one-dimensional people going about their business, their love lives. And another world: a twilight night world of neon and secrets, of secret dreams and deals, of different morals and different codes. At night these worlds cross and those from the world above of sun and light step down into the underworld to taste darkness, to take a neon bath: and those from the underworld sometimes step up into the living rooms and bedrooms of the seemingly respectable for a deal of drugs or sex, or just to add a little twilight glamour. It is then that we find that we are really, basically, the same, we just wear different coats. In the city we see glamour and tragedy in the glimpse of an eye, sometimes on either side of a street at the same time. As one aspiration is realised, another dream dies. Both have beauty.

When I was seventeen I started a mysterious journey through life – inspired by John Rechy's *City of Night* which became a bible. Inspired by *Our Lady of the Flowers* by Genet, and by the songs of Brel and Piaf. It is a journey through cities – London, New York, Las Vegas, Los Angeles, Barcelona, Rio, Bangkok, Berlin, Hamburg, St Petersburg, Beirut, Tokyo, Amsterdam, Paris and Rome. I have fallen in love with all of them on my visits, and all of them at sometime or another have become a setting for one of my songs: where the hustler is hero and the loser is saint, where the ugly is beautiful and the beautiful more beautiful, in the gutter where gold is found. In the gutter, but looking up at the stars. Stories of Johnny, the lost boy chasing the dragon to escape his world of dreams, where sometimes death is the only escape. In this world where the thief is prince I have always tried to remain naïve, like a child lost in the corrupted world, even though I know that you cannot be corrupted and innocent. I know I am not innocent.

So at night I walked Eighth Avenue in New York in the humid summer heat, drinking in the sounds and street magic, the hustling, the secret codes, the sign language, the greetings from the black hustlers and dealers careful not to display 'V for Victim' in neon on my forehead, looking at the floor, staring ahead and just glancing occasionally and casually, taking in the scene and gathering knowledge for street survival. Melting into shadows, avoiding direct eye contact and acting crazy under threat.

I came to London in my late teens, before I became a pop star. I immersed myself in the scene for a while, worked on the door of a clip joint, got to know the streets and the clubs and the street characters. When I became successful I was given so many keys to so many cities. People had listened to my songs and read the themes of my lyrics, so they knew where to take me and who to introduce me to. Prostitutes, hustlers, porn stars, strippers, gangsters, pimps, dominatrixes, transsexuals, madams, subculture celebrities, superstars and even Satan worshippers – they have all danced in and out of 'my beautiful twisted night.' In this book I have included some of my favourite songs, verse and poems of the past twenty years, on red light, the night, or city themes. Many have featured on record and each of my albums is represented here. I have also included one or two excerpts from early writings: 'Zazou' – a play performance about Johnny, a rent boy and his dark destructive relationship with Zazou, an androgynous teenage drag queen, and 'Twilights and Lowlifes', a cabaret collage of songs, films and performance. My early Super-8 films, like my epic 'Glamour in Squalor', filmed in 1977, are long lost. Only 'Teenage Vice and 'The Cat Food Woman', filmed in 1978, remain. It was during these early performances that I met David Ball and formed Soft Cell. My poems and experimentation fashioned themselves into a more pop/dance form and we became the first successful so-called 'electro-duo' in Britain.

Marc Almond
1998

early years

fun city
1978

I left my home
With a pain in my heart,
Not a word of goodbye
To the ones that I loved.
I'm taking a train
Away from the rain
To the lights and the smoke
I've got to find my own way now.

Fun City
To the London Experience
Fun City
To the London Experience
Backward
Forwards
Wearing out the corners
Fun City
Here's my inexperience

Have no feelings,
Have no sex,
Wonder who
To pick up next.
Playland Scandal,
Pocket weighs you down,
Machine handle
Goes down.
I lose all my money
Trying to make a killing –
Can't even make my fare back home.
So this is Fun City

Have no feelings,
Have no sex
Wonder who
To pick up next.

I tried to make friends,
Tried to make amends.
I sunk so low
That it's hard to climb out.

I've nowhere to live
But I've so much to give.
I've found the hard way
What life's all about.

Have no feelings,
Have no sex
Wonder who
To pick up next.

I'm all alone
And I'm lost
In this city,
Feeling degraded,
Being paraded.
I wanted love
And I thought
This was the way,
But I'm only young
And I'm often this wrong.

Have no feelings,
Have no sex
Wonder who
To pick up next.
Have no morals,
Have no innocence,
I'm quite straight –
Just playing for rent.

twilights and lowlifes
leeds 1978

Twilights and lowlifes,
Looking for the highlife.
Twilights and lowlifes,
Looking for the highlife.
See them in and out of shadows,
Sinking in the night life.
Watch them hide,
Slip and slide,
Faceless figures
Trying to keep their pride.

Twilights and lowlifes

Twilight in the daylight
Twilight in the daylight
When the sun goes in
Then they all crawl out.
Sink into a doorway and lurk about
Begging for a chance
To pick up a trade,
Number one in the down and out
    parade.
Twilights and lowlifes,
Looking for the highlife.

Twilights and lowlifes

When you see behind the bright
    bright lights
What's going on in the
Lust of the night –
A thousand pretty things
That'd made you sick,
Human ashtrays trying to turn a
    trick.
A man in a doorway has a hard
    hard heart,
A nice little boy,
And a drunken tart.

Twilights and lowlifes

A hand in hand
Is a minute of time,
A whisper in the ear
Is a photograph.
A promise in a doorway is a part in
    a film,
A hand in a pocket is a packet of
    pills.
Huge light,
Black light,
Time to kill.

Twilights and lowlifes
Hiding from the daylight,
Trying to find
The dream inside,
Trying to find
The peace of mind,
Trying to find a car
And a holiday.
Trying to find a lover,
Trying to find a mother,
Who, it doesn't matter –
One or the other.

Twilights and lowlifes

Surrounded by the stink of
    cigarettes
In a poolroom toilet
That'll make you retch,
Look in the mirror
In the yellow light
From the broken windows
Comes the light of the night.
Pull out the piece of paper
That holds your fun,

Down amongst the hankies and the
    chewing gum.
Kick the closet door open,
Afraid of what you see –
Kneel down and shut your eyes
In the sanctuary.
The more you see
In the cold cold light
You're out of danger and out of
    sight,
You take a bit –
Then a place to hide.
Try to involve
Your dream inside.

marc almond

the girl with the patent leather face

1980

(Look she's here again)
The girl with the patent leather face
Tears pictures out of magazines
Looks longingly at make-up ads
And glossy spreads of beauty
    queens.

The girl with the patent leather face
Sits in a darkened bedsit gloom.
She chains her door,
Squats on the floor
Lets no one into her room.

Two-faced baby
Shiny baby
Two-faced baby
Shiny baby

You can laugh,
Point at me –
They do it all the time.
But how would you
Like it if you
Had a face like mine?

The girl with the patent leather face
Is a psychopathic mental case –
A target for freaks and creeps,
A reject of the human race.
The girl with the patent leather face
Hangs around the mutant bars,
She tampers with machinery
So other beauties crash their cars.

Two-faced baby
Shiny shiny shiny baby
Two-faced baby

You can laugh,
Point at me –
They do it all the time.
But how would you
Like it if you
Had a face like mine?

I'm alone
And she's alone
And we should get together.
I'll never ask her
To remove
Her mask of patent leather.

Patent leather

If you kiss me,
Kiss me,

Kiss me shiny baby
With your lips of patent leather
And your cold cold eyes.

seedy films
1981

Sleazy city
Seedy films
Breathing so heavy,
Next to my neighbour –
Let's get acquainted.
Getting to know you,
Feeling sleazy
In sleepy sin city.

Sleazy city
Sleepy people
Down in your alleys,
Seems that anything goes:
Blue films flicker,
Hands of a stranger.
Getting to know you,
And I'm getting to like you.

Hey that's fine,
Got no time.
Meet me on Friday,
Down in Blue City.
Got no address
Just a telephone number –
Phone me tonight
And maybe we can talk dirty.

Sleazy city
Sleepy people
Down your alleys,
Seems that anything goes:
Blue films flicker,
Hands of a stranger.
Getting to know you,
And getting to like you.

Hey isn't that you on the screen?
Isn't that you on the screen?
(No that's not me.)

marc almond

heat
1982

It was the heat of the night I think
Or it could of been the effect of the
    drink,
But I had to brush away the flies
That started to collect
Around your eyes.
I've still the taste of the sweat and
    the dust.
You're still playing games
And abusing my trust.

In the heat of the night,
In the glow of the night,
It's the back and the bite
That's feeling all right.
Do you use up bodies like
    cigarettes?
Do you need them for ego?
Do you need them for sex?

It was the bite of the night gone
    wrong
And the effect of listening to
    negative songs,
Stuck in a love scene from 'Blood
    and Sand',
And the way the room keeps
    spinning around.
I've still the taste of the sweat and
    the dust.
You're still playing games and
    abusing my trust.

(Now I know what they mean
By looks can kill,
And they're having a strange effect
    on the way I feel).

In the heat of the night,
In the glow of the light,
It's the back and the bite
That's feeling all right.
Do you use up bodies like
    cigarettes?
Do you need them for ego?
Do you need them for sex?

And you're moaning about your
    wasted life,
Lying there listening to 'Spanish
    Eyes',
With the cups on the floor
And the plates in the sink
And a room full of smoke
And then you full of drink.
Your skin's going dry
And the colour of the sand,
Ignore the cigarette burning your
    hand.

baby doll

1982 new york

Baby doll
Is on her trapeze,
Wearing the smile
That she never sees.
Thinking of a dollar
As she tries to tease,
Thinking of a dollar
As she tries to tease.

Baby Doll Baby Doll

Time to play Sheba
On a wooden stage,
Taking off the clothes
That are grimy with age,
Rubbing down the skin
That is white and cold,
And the sticking plasters
That cover up the holes.
Stared at by a man
That would do her harm,
Needs to earn the money
That will feed his arm.
He promised you security,
Safe and warm.

They'll never know
The hurt that you feel inside,
The emptiness you try to hide.

I would melt your eyes
That are glassy and cold.
A nest for the future when
You grow old.

Baby Doll
Baby Doll
He'll never know
The hurt you feel inside,
The emptiness
You try to hide.

Take a tiny costume
From a pile of clothes,
Just a touch of glitter
But a lot of gold.
Pick on a failure –
Make his knees go weak,
Mouth open –
Eyes wide –
Fake your peak.

He'll wipe a line of dribble
Falling from his mouth.
Make your wages later
When you're back at his house.
Try to hide the mirror
'Cause it's never kind.
Kick start the heart
That's so hard to find.
Try to save the beauty
And to draw the line.
Bite your lip when you find it tough –
Continue to search
For a genuine love.

'Baby Doll' was inspired by watching a down-at-heel exotic dancer at the Baby Doll
lounge, a topless bar in New York. The song appeared on Soft Cell's *Art of Falling Apart*
album. A year later I went back to the bar and a dancer was dancing on the trapeze to the
song which was playing on a tape.

marc almond

numbers

inspired by the John Rechy book of the same name

1982

Numbers
Who's the person
That you woke up next to today?
If you were any older
Then you know
You'd have to pay your way.
Well maybe you do already,
But you make out they pay you.
Did you ask yourself
Where did life go wrong with you?

Numbers
Don't tell me your name –
I don't want to know –
And don't forget to take all
    reminders
When you go.
Good things have to end
And I was never any good at saying
    goodbye,
Because when I say goodbye
A silly thing happens,
And I always cry.

Numbers
You're looking so thin these days
Are you doing speed? (no numbers)
Have you seen yourself?
You're really going to seed.
Two in a night,
Five in a day,
And you never know their names –
Because names make a person real
And there's no real people in these
    games.

Numbers
Pass them on, pass them by,
Numbers
Never hold a good thing down for
    long.

Numbers
Throw 'em away like Kleenex.
Numbers
Pick them up and push them away.

Numbers
Until you wake one day
And find that you're a number.
Body one, body two
Body three, body four
Numbers

it's a mug's game

london 1982

Oh god it's another night,
And your head is feeling
Like a lump of lead.
You should never have drunk
Those party-fours,
You should of been home being
   good instead.

Ever been in a deja vu/and the end
is the same again/you ran out of
your silver thins/and you're trying
to be so high class/though you need
a bath and your hair's looking like
string/and though you're nearly
broke you end up paying for all the
drinks and you tell them 'Oh it's
nothing – there's a million where
those come from' and then you
whisper to your longest-suffering
friend, 'Please lend me a few quid'.

Oh god it's another day,
And your stomach's feeling
Like a blown-up balloon.
You should never have eaten that
   greasy food –
The doctor told you that chilli was
   bad for your blood

And you're standing at the chemist
(in Boots) coughing up your guts
like you're at death's door – all this
for a packet of Do-Do's/and the
assistant gives you a wink and you
turn bright red – it's at time like this
that you wish you were dead – and
you take the whole packet and you
feel like you've drunk a bottle of
bleach and you tell yourself 'Never,
never again … well, not until next
week anyway'/and you were never
one for holding drink and you
stagger off to the toilet and you
throw up like it was Christmas and
you miss the bowl and you hit your
shoes and there's no paper towels –
now what else can go wrong for
you/it's a choice between a cab fare
home and a packet of cigarettes and
the money sticks in the machine and
the manager says 'Tough shit –
drink up and leave.'

marc almond

Oh god it's another disease
And you just got rid of the last.
You were beginning to feel OK,
And the friends you gave it to
Were speaking to you again.

And you find yourself having sex in
the back of a car and the girl
underneath doesn't care who you
are and you're nearly there and she
still doesn't care and her chewing
gum is getting stuck in your
hair/And there's something wrong –
something that you forgot – oh shit,
you've forgotten the rubber and you
don't want a kid … well, deny it
was you – if your dad finds out then
he'll make you stay in and do your
homework and cut your hair and
wear your school uniform out in the
street – oh what a fate worse than
death/oh well he can't hit you, you
can hit him back and play your
records so loud – all the ones that
he especially hates – Deep Purple in
Rock, Led Zeppelin II – well even
you hate those/well on second
thoughts I think I'll go and live in
America because they earn more
money there and they can get away
with murder – Yeah!

Oh this is a mug's game.
I can't wait until I'm twenty-one
And I can tell them all to sod off.

やはり Vol. 4 から
お願いします。それから Vol. 0 ～ 3 までの
バックナンバーも お願いします。お忙しいところ
大変 恐縮でございます。

ASAKO KURIHARA

her imagination

She slips in and out
Of her dull imagination
That floats around the twilight of her
   tomb.
Clutching the little treasures
That represent a happy moment,
Displayed with sad affection
In her room.
But this life is a prison,
And it hurts to hear the children
   laughing
While they live their pretty little
   dreams.
And frozen all the while
Is a bitter little smile:
Nothing is really what it seems.

Like a silly little fool
You were left standing at the altar,
Hypnotised by the candles as they
   burn.
Pressed against the mirror,
Playing all your favourite film stars –
Ready for the camera
That would never never turn.
Push aside the curtain
Of your tiny garret window
And glare out at the narrow little
   world.
You were in your wedding dress –
Great Expectations,
More or less.
Playing with your dolls
Like any ordinary girl.

Candle light
Candle bright
Won't you light my way tonight?

Now it's the futile bitter feelings
That clutch you in the middle –
You were never really given a
   chance –
And the spite that jabs your mind
Hides a heart that's really warm and
   kind,
And the pulse that races
With each over-inquisitive glance.
You were always the outsider,
And they set you up at childhood
To be just another cuddly toy.
And they whisper on the street
When the street-corner gossips
   meet:
The woman on the fourth floor –
He was such a happy boy.

Candle light
Candle bright
Won't you light my way tonight?

untitled

1982

Out on the street again
Playing with the rain,
And a friend is walking away.
Life in a strange hotel
And an endless hell,
Thinking of things
I wanted to say.
We overplayed the game
And we're playing with pain,
And the black inside
Is turning white with the rain.

And the smiles are down,
And the feelings are fine,
It's hard to make the sun shine.

It's such a shame
When I'm out in the rain.
All the curtains are closed,
It's a sad scene I know.
I try not to care
That time's going nowhere –
See it slide down the drain –
Wash away with the rain.

I'm walking in the night
And I feel
Like a tiger loose in a room full of
    fools.
And it's hurting inside,
This feeling of pride,
Looking for somewhere to run and
    hide.
Life's a merry-go-round,
It's the same old sad sound,
And it's happened again
As it happened before.

And the smiles are down
And the feelings are fine,
It's hard to make the sun shine.

It's such a shame
When I'm out in the rain.
All the curtains are closed,
It's a sad scene I know.
I try not to care
That times going nowhere –
See it slide down the drain –
Wash away with the rain.

Only the lonely,
Only the lonely,
Need to be lonely,
Love to be lonely.

marc almond

little rough rhinestone

1983

Little rough rhinestone
Where did your love go today?
Sometimes you think
You had none to start with anyway.

You will lose those deep pools,
And the blues will cloud up
Your frightened little eyes.
And the cold comes to claim you
    inside.

You sit writing letters to imaginary
    friends
That you left behind in your mind,
The deep dark red doorways
Call to a limbo of loneliness
Where a million rhinestones sit and
    cry.

I never knew sorrow
Could hit me this way,
I once had a friend
But he moved away.
And even my mother,
When she turned on me,
Couldn't put emotion
Like this in me.

Fist into glass into head –
Someone else's head.
They beat you up so badly
That your eyes
Show the look of the nearly dead.
The wagon will come and scoop up
What's left of the sorry debris
And you'll take the place
Of a hundred other little Johnnys
That went the very same way.

I never knew sorrow
Could hit me this way,
I once had a friend
But he moved away.
And even my mother,
When she turned on me,
Couldn't put emotion
Like this in me.

Then screaming out loud –
He ran crashing through the crowd
He ran crashing through the crowd
He ran crashing through the crowd
Screaming:
'God if you're up there
I need you
Where are you?
I need you.
Where are you
When I need you?'

where was your heart

(when you needed it most)

1983

You're time-wasting again
Biting your nails like you were
    sixteen,
Putting up your little walls
When emotion's around.
Leave your little heart
In the lost and found.
Your friends would die laughing
If they saw you this way,
Even though they cry the same
Tears every day.
Where was your heart
When you needed it most?
Hand in hand
With your innocence,
Gave up the ghost.

But it doesn't do to tell
You're at your best
When you're living hell –
Just put on your hard face
You know you do that so well.
Thank God you wore
Your waterproof make-up today,
And who gives a damn about him
    anyway?
To him you're a body
And to hell with the mind,
But you get the same stick
From his type all the time.
Just a couple of drinks
And they've got you tonight,
And you know the sad thing
Is that they're often right.

Where was your heart
When you needed it most?
Hand in hand with your innocence,
Gave up the ghost.

They take hold of your heart
And they spit it right out,
Make a show of their conquests
When their friends are about.
Your ego deflated,
You gave up the fight
And became the good time
Had by all every night.

And where was your heart
When you needed it most?
Hand in hand with your innocence,
Gave up the ghost.

No comfort of beds
Or the softness of sheets,
Just the back of a car,
Sprawled across the back seats.
And he just won't give up
Till he's messed up your head –
A dish in the disco
But a pig in the bed.
So you build up a false love affair
    anyway –
Photocopy soap opera stories all
    day –
Where it all ends up fine.
And it all ends in church
And the girl looks like you
And she never really gets hurt.

Where was your heart
When you needed it most?
Hand in hand with your innocence,
Gave up the ghost.

marc almond

surrender to a stranger
1983

Lonely
I'd like to drown me in my coffee,
Passing hours with cappuccinos,
Sitting framed in the window.
Lonely
I sit here acting like I'm reading –
I'm reading minds
And sadly dreaming
There's some of me left to believe in.

Surrender
Surrender

That businessman smell
Found in one-night hotels:
The sheets are unwashed,
From the stories they tell,
Tobacco and sweat
And initials in dust.
The man at the desk
Throws you looks of disgust.
Soon I'll try hard to lose you,
Drown you in my cappuccino.

Surrender
Surrender

Sodom and Gommorrah
Come tomorrow
I won't know you from Adam or Eve.
Look me in the eyes
And tell me you love me
Once, before you leave.

Surrender
Surrender

excerpt from 'zazou'

Zazou was my second performance show, the first being *The Vampire Cat*. It was written and performed in 1976–77 and was about a nihilistic relationship between a rent boy and a drag queen.

BLUE HEAVEN NARRATIVE

There is no neon, no plaque, no notice at all to advertise Blue Heaven, you have to go through an insignificant doorway beside a barber's shop, up a staircase and ring on the bell. The door is opened by two burly heavyweights who scan up and down for signs of trouble. It is like a scene from the American 1930s depression. You pay your entrance to the freak show then take your place among the exhibits. A mottled selection of choice human ashtrays who drape themselves around the bar and stairway, bent broken miserable dummies searching, for a body, anybody … They are miserable flotsam and jetsam, bottom-of-the-bin angels putting on a brave face. As each sexual encounter turns out to be a disaster they will revel in the hand-over-heart drama and return to their bedsits, Valium and pet cat. Zazou feels at home here. The décor is delightful, dark purple walls on which glitter a galaxy of appliqué stars cut out of silver foil and pasted at random. Little tables clutter around a postage-stamp dance floor that throbs with a illuminated back drop and an amplified transistor radio. They call it a disco. Yes, there are plenty of dark corners for a quick flirt with oral sex. A lump of a queen with a badly-positioned wig seems to be doing just that and with every bob of the head the wig threatens more and more to reveal its wearer. The creature has finished, she wipes her mouth and swigs from her pint of bitter.

Two heavy lesbians who have been grappling on the dance floor plonk themselves down near to Zazou.

'Hi, Zaz', says one mountain of a lesbian with a big grin and a slap that sends Zazou's vodka and orange over the queen at the next table. 'Hey, guess what?' The lesbian nudges Zazou 'What?' smiles Zazou politely.

'I've just had some tattoos done', she pulls open her donkey jacket revealing a flattish chest.

On one tit was carved 'Mild', the other 'Bitter'. 'Where's the lager?' asks Zazou wishing as soon as she'd said it that she'd never asked.

The lesbian grins and winks.

Zazou spies Johnny over in a corner chatting to a female form. She watches for a while, a knot in her stomach. Johnny puts his arm around the female who snuggles into Johnny. Johnny kisses her on the cheek lightly then launches a full assault on her mouth. The knot in Zazou's stomach nearly strangles her intestines and she breaks out in a cold sweat ... Zazou orders a double vodka and knocks it back, another and knocks it back. The silver stars circle round and around the ceiling and the flashing disco lights and the hypnotic sounds lure her to the dance floor.

All the people have gone, the club is swimming with a blue haze that splits up the cigarette smoke into beams. There is a little rustle of applause and suddenly from nowhere a saxophone starts playing the blues. Zazou is wearing a short black frock, simple and slightly frayed around the edges. She is barefoot, her black hair tousled and mascara blurred around the eyes. Like Piaf. In the centre of the dance floor is one solitary microphone illuminated by a single cruel spotlight. Zazou walks over to it and grasps it with both hands, she throws her head back and her hands up: 'This is a song inspired by Shirley Bassey'.

Strange men strange hotels:
I have been around.
Strange men strange hotels:
I have tried them all,
Suffered all their comforts,
A new one
Round each corner.
Strange men,
Strange hotels:
I know which ones are warmer.
Strange men,
Strange hotels:
A way of earning money.
Some are cruel,
Some are kind:
All are necessary.

Anne Tilby as Johnnie and
Marc as Zazou

the boys
1978

Hello darling / my friend fancies you … No she does … No he does / hello dear / like your hair / bursts of giggles / shrieks. The Dilly arches are an exotic paradise of screaming parrots flapping their features and pouting. Black boy / girl / good make up sickly shirt, I'd think it was class if I hadn't seen him/her wearing the same shirt yesterday and the day before. He bitches and turns his head quickly. White boy plucks his eyebrows badly needs a lesson in cosmetics / nice jacket, shame about the shoes. White boy – streaky hair / gone mad with the tanfastic / won't you learn it won't hide acne? Must have scored well, leather trousers / good make. Their words become harsh ear-grating shrieks. I see punters shying away with looks of distaste. For god's sake scatter / here comes Bill. Flock of parrots flap away. The stone of the arches come to life as chameleons slink out of the shadow. Stern faces young but … hustler outfits / no queers these babies or so they'll tell you as they bite the pillow. Favourite lines:

My girlfriend's pregnant	Inside
Bashed a cop	Robbed a bank
Wanted	My girl
Get married	Girl
Girlfriend	I'm twenty-one
My girlfriend	

White boy – tattoos / self-penned / ratty jeans, faded T-shirt, punky hair, seen it all / done it all look. Black boy, beige trousers, fairly clean, new shoes, good score, ricochet eyes. Not quite seen-it-all, certainly won't-do-it-all look. Half-caste boy, white jacket, got some taste in his packaging, looks clean. Do I smell innocence? Hasn't seen it all but says he has; says he won't do it all but if desperate for a bed will swallow the world.

Scatter here comes Bill.

Foxes dance with the fighters, it's a real fashion show. Round and round on the Wurlitzer meat rack. The foxes – mother rat bag the walking dead, 69 years and she doesn't know of any other way – Rose who stood up in court charged with interference with a minor and spoke bravely to the judge, 'A boy? I don't want a boy, what would I do with that, I want a man, something like so' (indicates a huge length) 'not something like this' (crooks her little finger). Islington Ada and Davinia who is hunting for a leather boy, her favourite game is to get a boy with a bike, she makes the boy bring the bike into the flat and rev it up while she sits astride the back, holding on to the throttle ... like Boadicea.

Airport Lil also known as a Tightfist Tessie ... A fiver take it or leave it, and they have to be special to get that much. Foxes and fighters dance. Walk a few paces / stop / glance back / walk back a few paces / smile / approach each other / stop / bargain / nod or shakes of the head / pause / walk on. Eyes are everywhere / boys crawl out of the tiles / boys crawl out of the stone / boys crawl out of the doorways one there ... someone there ... where'd he go? Don't touch him, girl he'll wet your bed. Don't touch him, girl he'll want 30 before you even start.

Don't touch him, girl he's a rip-off, stole my razor.

Don't touch him, I don't like the company he keeps.

Don't touch him, girl he's dead meat.

Don't touch him, he's one of Eddie's Boys.

'You know' says Rose 'I picked up a Vietnamese boy yesterday. One of the Boat People. I said to him "Would you like to come for a coffee?" "Oh no", he said "I ...". "Nonsense", I said, "come along" and I dragged him off by the arm. Later on in my flat after we'd finished he dug deep into his pocket. "I haven't got much to pay you", he said shyly. "Oh make it my pleasure" I laughed. Honestly he thought I was an old prostitute. Makes a change for them to pay you.' She shrieked with laughter joined by the gaggle of old punters flapping wildly. Oh god look at those screaming cows.

Airport Lil points to the pouting parrots. A young dark boy pirouettes in a pair of shorts. He wags his arse at an old queen who nearly chokes on her teeth.

The state of that and the price of bacon.

A line of tigers on the shop railings make a misery chain. They gather on one side the parrots on another – the foxes stand in the middle – the tableau is shattered.

Scatter / here comes Bill.

the boys

The singer sings
The meat rack crowded with
    vegetarian diners,
The arches littered with foxes and
    fighters.
Five fingers catch my sight,
Gold glints in neon light.
Thinks:
I could do better, I could do worse.

(Excuse)
I'm sorry I am with a friend.
I'm sorry I have commitments.
(he said) I'm Persian, you can see.
(thinks) In oil wells he must be –
Show me proof and then we'll see.
(he said) I will give you one
    hundred pounds
If you will come with me (cash
    before you start).
(thinks) One hundred lovely
    pounds,
How wonderful that sounds.
And we'll do what you decide
(said he)

I'll do it, I said to him eagerly,
My fingers feverish, my colours
    running.

How far?, I said
(he said) Don't worry, follow me
To Ealing out of the city.
It was then I began to worry.
We arrived in Ealing,
A place for the grey.

He staggered, (drunk) swearing at
    passers by.

(I said) Don't attract attention.
(he said) Why?
Well take a look at me,
I'm dressed eccentrically
And a fist in the face is no fun.

We at last arrived at a semi-
    detached,
It was *très sordide*.
I began to curse at my greed.
(thinks) I hope he's got money
Or he'll get nothing from me.
It was too late now I had missed the
    last tube.

In a filthy room I realised my
    mistake:
(I said) Show me your money,
Don't worry (he said).
I got down on my knees.
Kiss it, kiss it, kiss it please,
I tried my best (emptily).

A hundred pounds? – not a hundred
    pence did he give me,
I felt green and greasy from olive
    oil.

He threw me in the street,
He laughed and called me shit.
He got his ... and I got mine.

Taxi!!
Round each corner,
Strange men, strange hotels,
I know which ones are warmer.
Strange men, strange hotels,
A way of earning money.
Some are cruel,
Some are kind,
All are necessary.

marc almond

a beautiful
twisted night

a beautiful twisted night

1996

On a beautiful twisted night,
Taking pleasure of the red-light life,
Drinking in the street magic,
Dancing down the night's alleys,
Like an invisible dreamer.

Like saints in the underworld,
Dipping into sleepy girls
On the Reeperbahn past midnight,
On the street of a thousand pleasures –
Taking the treasures
And staying alive.

In a town way past its prime,
Somewhere sordid and sublime–
Peepshows, bedshows, old arcades –
Seasoned hookers play charades
And dress in nylon
Just to tantalise us.

Children in a world of glue,
Lips of blue,
Not much to do but lose themselves.
Escorts dance in lycra shorts,
Snorting coke off toilet lids.
Their harsh retorts
Bring us down to earth,
While dreaming up
Delicious ways to scandalise us.

deep night

Lately I've been having dreams,
strange kind of dreams,
Beautiful dreams,
In the deep night.
Sleep, an uneasy sleep,
The real and the unreal –
Hallucinations creep upon me.

Deep night,
In the deep night.

Take a walk on the street
And the heat is making the neon
    swim
In the deep night.
Police cars and sirens,
Explosions and light,
Sounds of passion –
Guns and love –
In the deep night.

Deep night,
In the deep night.

I'll follow the moon
Over the hill where
Tomorrow still sleeps.
The sky full of pearls,
The streets full of girls
Who will understand.

In the deep night

Lately I've been having dreams,
Strange kind of dreams,
Beautiful dreams,
In the deep night.

This night will never be through
Until someone can fill my time
And make me forget
The dreams I dream of you.
I'm wishing each kiss was mine,
And desire,

Deep night,
In the deep night.

There's love in the motion,
Love in the sound,
Of the deep night.
If love was an ocean
I would be drowned
In the deep night.

I'm dreaming of being in love –

Hold me in your arms,
Hold me tight,
I'm afraid of the dark.
And the deep night.

oily black limousine
1985

Me and my lover
Out taking the night
In an oily black limousine,
The rain melting the windows
And we deep in seductive sleep,
Late night jazz
Slow sliding away
To the timeless tune,
Time we found things to say
Like is love here to stay?
(No it's sliding away.)

Me and my lover
Out owning the night
Empty wet streets a-shimmering,
Neon night lights a-glimmering,
Slow sliding away.
Now we talk
About stupid things
Like is love here to stay?
(No it's sliding away.)

Sliding, sliding
In and out of the shadows,
Chasing my heart
On a yawning boulevard
To nowhere.

madame de la luna
1990

She's in my veins,
Gold in my veins,
She is my pain, and my joy,
Time and again,
Waxing and waning,
I am insane for la Luna,
Madame de la Luna.

When she is sleepy
She's creepy, mysterious and
    wicked.
When she is full
She is full of promise and joy,
Beaming her smile all the while
Across heaven's horizons,
Weaving her dreams into hearts of
    lonely boys.

But when I'm under the moon with
    you,
I'm in heaven.
When I'm under the moon with
    you,
I'm in heaven.

She'll bring out the killer
Bring out the lover

She loves a tyrant, a pirate, a
    dreamer, a crook and a liar,
A joker, a trickster, romancer, a
    dancer and fool.
Cold as the frost but in her heart is
    a fire
Hanging around the dark throat of
    the
Night like a jewel.

But when I'm under the moon with
   you,
I'm in heaven.
When I'm under the moon with
   you,
I'm in heaven.

Moon moon, delirious moon,
Alone in the blue
Like a silver balloon.
Moon, silver delirious moon
Dancing a waltz
To a lunatic's tune.
Madame de la Luna,
Bewitching is she –
I cannot live without her.
She's scattering stars,
Dancing with Mars.
Cheek to cheek
With La Luna.
Cheek to cheek
With la Luna.

Madame de la Luna,
She sings as she brings in the
   harvest.
She pulls out her tongue
At the cruel Ethiopian sun
When she's hiding, the dark
can bring a terrible vengeance,
A pounce in the shadows,
A moment alone with a gun.

Adrift on a sea of indigo silk,
Passionate like an Arabian torch,
Enticing two lovers to jump off a
   bridge,
Changing the man into the wolf.
Sometimes she's a terrible flirt

Causing mischief and mayhem
wherever she can.
Sometimes she's a woman that
   hurts,
Sometimes she is a man
Encouraging drunks to sing coarse
   serenades,
Lighting the way for the young
   renegades.

But when I'm under the moon with
   you,
I'm in heaven.
When I'm under the moon with
   you,
I'm in heaven.

She says better times are gonna
   come soon:
Trust in the moon,
Trust in the moon.

marc almond

night and no morning

1990

Night and no morning,
Day and no dawning,
And the tears that keep falling
Over me.
Dream with no ending,
Darkness descending,
And the years that keep calling
Out to me.

And soon comes the morning sun
Exposing my desires,
And then my heart will die,
My eyes will burn as I start to cry.
Eyes that seem only to weep,
Eyes that reveal a fear,
Where should be only sleep.
A fear tomorrow may find me here,
I push my tired body on,
In keeping the dawn at bay,
Afraid of what I've become.
Afraid of another day,
And soft is the rain on my face.
Lady Night weaves her magic spell
Hiding that which I fear –
The face I knew only so well.

Night and no morning,
Day and no dawning,
And the tears that keep falling
Over me.
Endlessly searching,
My hunger returning,
Loneliness burning
Into me.

If I believed in God
I'd pray for the dawn to stay away
For as the dawn awakes
This light will flicker, flicker and
    die.
Eyes that are hungry as mine,
Eyes that are desperate as mine,
We look and we recognise
Both seeing something we despise.

My eyes have seen tomorrow.
My eyes have seen the truth,
The all-revealing eyes:
Eyes that once burned, burned with
    youth.
Eyes will reveal what is true,
Eyes that look deep, deep in mine,
Eyes that belonged to someone I
    love.
Those eyes belong to someone like
    you.

indigo blue
london 1985

Indigo blue
Under a wicked red moon,
Body primed,
Deep in crime,
Here's thinking of you.
Soft the sound
Of lips against the ground.
Death wore chinchilla,
Catch me a killer –
Paint me the town.

Still time,
All's fine.
Shivering dreams,
Blood line,
Moonshine,
Brittle beams.

Love paint me blue –
Indigo colouring you.
Fevered brow,
Time is now –
The things love makes us do.
Fire brights the room
Where candles neglect the gloom,
Aura lights
Bathe the night,
Here's thinking of you.
Still time,
All's fine,
Shivering dreams,
Blood line,
Moonshine,
Brittle beams,

Another soul goes to the stars
Another soul goes to the stars
To the stars.

marc almond

i've never seen your face

london 1990

Sometimes we touch,
Sometimes we kiss,
Sometimes we just look
In spiritual bliss.
In warmth or heat,
In sound or vision,
We like to come
To some decision.
Under the moon
In the dark,
Down in the street,
In the park.
In threat of law,
In sweat of fear,
I'd risk it all
To have you near.

I've never seen your face
But I'm longing for the time
When we don't have to hide
Anymore.

We swap phone numbers
But we never call;
Of real excuses
We've none at all.

Though good intentions
Are on our mind
We may not like
What we might find.
We hold emotion
Well in check,
No words of love
Just words of sex.
So much to say,
So much held back,
We don't surrender,
We just attack.

I've never seen your face
But I'm longing for the time
When we don't have to hide
Anymore.

Light the candle,
Burn a fuse,
It's now or never,
Win or lose.
To have and hold,
To give and take,
Through thick and thin,
Make or break.

I've never seen your face
But I'm longing for the time
When we don't have to hide
Anymore,
Anymore.

beautiful twisted night   43

amnesia nights

1991

Those amnesia nights
On the edge of sleep,
You were there for real
While I was just a dream.
Lips just touching,
Fingers entwined,
Sentimental music,
Sentimental rhymes.

Those amnesia nights
Lost in the city lights,
You floating round me like
A gentle satellite.
I try to catch you
But you disappear –
Maybe you're the dream
And I'm really here.

But in a twilight world
Between despair and pain
We stood waiting for
A carnival refrain.
A cavalcade of clowns,
Fragile dancers in their sequinned
    gowns,
Painted horses with gilded manes –
But they never came.

Those amnesia nights
Spent in an open car,
Somewhere in my mind
Laughing at the stars.
Love's magic weaving
Its deceptions,
Future plans are full
Of good intentions.

Those amnesia nights
Of mist and fairy dust,
Pouring out our hearts
Foundations built on trust.
We said all the things
That lovers say they feel
And you made me believe
That it was all for real.

But in a barren land
That thirsts for lovers' tears,
We waited in the line
Of eternal years
That lead to heaven's door.
But heaven disappeared
Now I see it all:
Heaven was already here.

Those amnesia nights
In a forgotten daze,
Pictures taking shape
In a smoking haze.
When passion is new
And walking hand in hand,
Staking claim
On undiscovered land.

It's becoming clear
I see it now, I find
Those amnesia nights
Were really in my mind.
And now it seems
The laughter and the tears were
    real.
Is love just a passing emotion
That everybody feels?

marc almond

so what's tonight?

1993

I apply my face,
Stake out a friendly space.
Chasing dark horses away,
I rejoin the race,
Dance at my lonely pace.
No more dark horses I say,
Where did they go?
Nothing left to show
And long is the night
Alone.

So what's tonight?
Tired words and shallow games,
Love by another name.
My eyes shut tight,
No not tonight.

I pick out the face,
Assault the task.
I always ask,
So what's tonight?

No taste I ever tried before,
The simple things that I adore.
Life is a wheel,
Repeated feelings
Always leave you wanting more,

Somewhere you know
You've been before.
I head for home,
Take time to pray,
Maybe dark horses
Can stay
Another day,
Another night.
And still I say,
So what's tonight?

the scarlet bedroom

(original lyrics) 1996

Come into the scarlet bedroom
And maybe stay the night,
Sink among the satin sheets
In dissolute delight.
Just a little touch of darkness
A subtle hint of light.
You can call me bad,
Call me heartless,
But please call me tonight.
It's truly
Star-spangled fabulous lover
In the red bedroom.
In the red bedroom,
Gonna open up your eyes to a little
    life,
Come and taste something
    delicious,
Prepare for your demise,
Never ever repetitious,
Always a surprise,
Just a little touch of sadness,
A little second sight.
Come into my world of madness,
Come and spend the night.
It's truly
Star spangled fabulous lover
In the red bedroom.
In the red bedroom,
You won't be getting out alive.

Take me to your burlesque show,
I want to be in your show.
It's gonna be monumental.
Come and be my movie star,
You can do the striptease
In my new continental hot blue
    movie,
We could film it in my scarlet
    bedroom.

Try a little tender moment
But don't let it suffice –
Why be happy with vanilla
When you can have the spice?
Sugar-coated innocence
Is something not too nice.
Call me cruel or call me callous
But please call me tonight.
It's truly
Star-spangled fabulous lover,
In the red bedroom,
I mean the dead red room.
Hold me hard and kiss your life
    goodbye.

sleepwalker

(original lyrics) 1997

Love, love
Where did it go?
Gone to a land
Of satin and snow,
Long gone
Like the look on your face,
Lost in your box
Of feathers and lace.

A drifter,
A dreamer,
In a shady world of disbelieving
Love seemed to be always leaving,
Comatosed to walk the ceiling,
Numb and never feeling.
Doesn't the city
Look so pretty
In a late-night lazy sort of way?

Sleepwalker,
Dream talker,
Turning all your days around,
Floating through life
Like a fabulous phantom
In a somnambulistic decay.

Love, love
Where did it go?
Gone to a land
Of satin and snow,
Long gone
Like that look on your face,
Into your box
Of feathers and lace.
You were a liar,
You were a talker,
When emotions you were thieving.
Love seemed to be always leaving,
Barely breathing,
Dream believing,
For a lost love always grieving.

Doesn't the city
Look so pretty
In a late-night, lazy sort of way?

Sleepwalker,
Dream talker,
Throwing all your days away,
Floating through life
Like a fabulous phantom
In a somnambulistic decay.

Tears run down your paralysed face,
Your head a confusion of
    snowflakes and mace,
Lost on a sea
Of jelly and glue,
Half-lit illusions and lace.

mysterious lover

1991

Mysterious lover:
I know nothing about you
And what I know
I don't want to know,
I hoped I'd be part
Of your passing adventure,
But you stayed too long
And now I don't want you to go.

But you're here in my heart
Putting fear in my soul –
It's my old friend desire,
My mysterious lover,
My mysterious lover.

Mysterious lover:
Who will you be in the morning?
Lover or stranger?
I don't want to know –
I just want to be part
Of your passing adventure,
But I keep resisting
On insisting you go.

But you're here in my heart,
Putting fear in my soul –
It's my old friend desire.

My mysterious lover
My mysterious lover

You could come back to haunt me,
You could come back to hate me,
You could come back to taunt me
With somebody new.

So will we end up lovers or
   strangers
By the morning
When the yearning is through?

I just want to be part of
Your passing adventure,
Love's great adventure,
Love's great adventure.

brewer street blues

1982

The cold came in this morning,
Blew the ash clean out of the tray
And the sound of my record player
Ushers in the dawn of the day.
The dust cart is rattling down the street
Picking up bin bags on the way
Heard a prostitute wailing
That every guy she meets must be gay.
She hasn't made a penny
And has a month of bills to pay,
She hits out at the cruisers
And the dust cart knocks her out the way.
There's an outpost on the corner,
It calls itself the Coffee Pot café,
There's a young kid in the window
Trying to hide his face out the way.
He pushes away the time wasters,
He's got to find a punter to pay.

There's a crowd outside the peep show –
They've come down to Soho for the day –
They're screaming and they're shouting
At the clippers taunting.

I wish the dust cart would
Take them all away.

stars falling

catch a fallen star
1983

Black rings round your eyes
And you're spewing your lies
That you know is your old routine,
Spilling your drink with a nudge
    and a wink
As you joke about people you've
    been,
Smoking your cigarette
Down to the butt
And your teeth are as black as the
    tar.
You tell them at sex
You're a stud in the bed
As you hang for your life on the bar
And you see your own peak
On the top of a mountain
Of bodies you trod on to get there.
Shit on me,
Shit on her.
Shit on you in the end
And they won't even lend you the
    bus fare.
And you're boring the pants off the
    tart on the dance floor
As you tell her the person you once
    were.
She just sees you as trash
But she creams at the cash
That you might pay
Just to grope her.

And this town is a pot-pourri of
    disease:
You can smell the herpes
From the scum-fucking fucks
That hang round the same
Suckers each midnight.
You were being your photo
And spouting your promo,
Flicking back your limp quiff
That's as limp as your dick,
Irritating your greedy cross eyesight
Oh Christ.

And you're greasing up now
To the greedy old cow
You would sell out your mother
And besides,
You've a sell-out assured,
You were always a whore.
And you've always been taken
    for long rides,
At the smell of the bribe
You go jelly inside
As you step up the gold ladder to
    big time.
Kick them on the way up,
Kick you on the way down,
(And you'll meet them all again in
    good time).
Your friend is the 'yes' man
Who sits by your side
With his hand in your pocket all the
    time.
And he's messing your head,
Tries to get you in bed
(Well it's all masturbation of a
    kind).

What you earn heaven knows,
Goes straight up your nose
And you strangle your health in the
    end.
And you're blinded by bull
And you're really so full
It's driving you straight round the
    bend.
And you're told that a smile
is so worth your while,
It's what 'yes' men call diplomacy –
It'll get you the goal
But while losing the soul
You're forgetting the quality,
And you heave on your drink
As you're starting to think
That all that shines
May not be lamé
But a cheap substitute
That'll give you the boot.
You're just a stiff at a funeral party
And you slouch on the bar
With your arm in the beer
Wearing yesterday's
Mascara today,
And it runs when you cry
About living a lie
And the lie's starting to fade away,
Fade away …
Fade away …

your aura
1983

Sitting alone in the twilight of your
      room
With your face staring at the wall,
Playing with reminders of a
      yesteryear persona
That hasn't got a place at all.
You were in love with the caress of
      a camera
And I was in love with you,
Now the mirror's dimmed and
      cracked,
Like your aura and your glamour,
Makes the legend easier to live
      through.

And I once loved a smile
And I once dreamed a look,
I collected your memories too.
Now the eyes hold the flame
And your face holds the pain,
As you try to live your legend
      through.

It's so sad,
You never gave in smiling –
Ageing to an art –
Wishing we could be together
When we only grow apart.

Life behind the shades,
It's a life all in the mind
With no place in the living at all.
You died with the dreams
And, so it seems,
With imagination's downfall.
Keep the whispers,
Excite the adoration
That glows around the image of
      you,
With a kiss to the screen
As you play out the scene,
As you try to live your legend
      through.

And I once loved a smile
And I once dreamed a look,
I collected your memories too.
Now the eyes hold the flame
And your face holds the pain,
As you try to live your legend
      through.

It's so sad,
You never gave in smiling –
Ageing to an art –
Wishing we could be together
When we only grow apart.

marc almond

marlena's bed

1996

Marlena's bed
Where kings reclined,
Is filled with crisps
And orange rind.
No one knows
Quite what they'll find
In Marlena's bed.
There she sits
Empress divine,
Reminder of
More glamourous times
And across a faded photo
Signs, Marlena.

Marlena's bed,
Once satin bliss,
Has bowls for shit
And bowls for piss.
Sometimes so drunk
She aims to miss
And leaves a golden
Thread across the bedsheet.
Her phone
A line to her dominion,
She calls her past
To give opinion,
A broken voice
From one blue fallen angel.

Marlena's bed
A linen shrine
To tainted thoughts
And delicious crimes
Legend frozen
Caught in time
Preserving an illusion
Her face a bitter mask of truth
Scorning those
Who owe her youth
She fiercely guards her secret
For our pleasure.

Marlena's bed
Where she contains
The shock of fame
Long gone insane
Parades of pills
And shots to kill the pain
Of being Marlena
And though we know
We do not see
How age has dealt a legend cruelly
We caress our magic
And we thank Marlena.

sal mineo

1996

Sal Mineo
Murdered on the lawn,
Darkened life
So rudely torn,
Small and dark-eyed
Star forlorn,
Sweet Sal Mineo.

Sal Mineo
A broken gem,
Secret life of S&M;
Hollywood
Took all the good
From sweet Sal Mineo.

Sal Mineo
Loved rebel James
Who told him
About darker games
And drugs that took
The youthful look
From sweet Sal Mineo.

Sal Mineo
Murdered on the lawn,
Lay in blood
Where legend is born,
But soon forgotten
By the dawn
Sweet Sal Mineo.

a diva on a downward spiral

1992

Out every night
With diamonds and dare –
Fighting the fight
Of glamour and glare,
Where every bartender
Helps you to sink
In final surrender
To drama and drink.
You crawled
From gutter to glitter,
They made you a star
But you're drowning your sorrows
Each night in the bar.

Out every night
Kissing the guys,
Drowning in drink
And drugged to the eyes.
From Bradford to Brandy,
Martini to Mars,
Lurex to lamé.
Now one of the stars
From Vauxhall to Vegas,
They made you a name,
But inside you're lonely,
Lonely with fame.

Out every night
With hundreds of guys,
The world knows your name
But you're empty inside.
Nobody cares,
Nobody hears,
Your cocktail tonight
Is vodka and tears.

saint judy
1985

Saint Judy
She's staggering across the floor,
Saint Judy
Behaving like a whore,
Saint Judy
She's giving it all the tears.
She tears her dress,
Looks a mess.
Well I've wanted to do it for years,
Well I've wanted to do it for years.

Now I had a dream –
Well more a fantasy –
Kip Noll, John Holmes and me
All in bed we were going OTT,
What a sight to see,
What a sight to see.

Well a diva a day
Keeps the boredom away
I love 'em when they throw up their
    arms
And they bathe in that applause
Shouting
Screaming
Singing
Stamping
Slamming hotel doors.
Champagne chilled
And the pills well spilled,
All wide eyes
And overkill.

Minks
The drinks
The curves
The kinks
Always acts before she thinks,
Well that's what you call a star,
    boys,
That's what you call a star.
Too many of my skeletons
In other people's closets,
Too many people taking without
Leaving deposits,
Too many people bringing me down
Bringing me down,

Well they may find me on a hotel
    floor,
High heels in a pool of gore,
Curtains closed
And a bolted door
Breaking every law.

And if I die before I wake up
I pray the Lord don't smudge my
    make-up.
The dress will be fine when the hem
    I take up,
The dress will fit just fine.

Sometimes I feel like a moral-less
    child,
Sometimes I feel that I've gone too
    wild,
Spilled my guts,
Done myself in,
Died for a multitude of sins.
It feels good to die for your sins,
So good, boys.

Well let's all put on our sequinned
    dresses
And end it all in tears,
Let's all holler and beat our breasts
Ending it all in tears,
Christ I've wanted to do this for
    years.

Saint Judy
What are we going to wear?
Saint Judy
Our souls we're gonna bare.
Saint Judy
She's squeezing out those tears,
She tears her dress,
Looks a mess –
Christ I've wanted to do this for
    years.

dehumanise

new york 1983

Dehumanise
These human eyes,
They come to watch me
Fall into the pit.

Who would think
This celebrated face
Of yesteryear
Would sit here
Strapped into a bath,
What a laugh.

Dehumanise,
Who would think
Such elegance
Would straddle such a wicked
    fence?
They come to watch me
Fall off stage,
A cripple
Bent with dope and age,
To see me
Fly into uncontrollable rages.

Dehumanise
These tearful eyes.
They know I cannot hold myself,
They have me
Strapped on a commode
To humour me
As I corrode slowly.
Remember me the way I was,
Remember us the way we were.

Dehumanise,
They put a plug into my mouth,
Giggle as I jerk about
Driving all my demons out.
Dehumanise
These dead eyes,
There but for the grace of God
Go I.

marc almond

queen of heaven

1996

Blonde fire,
Heavenly desire,
Venus on a silver stage,
Diamanté all the rage.
In her universe
Alone,
With her silicone.
Way back in another age,
Men would spend their final wage
On one kiss
From her lips.

She took the step
From the photo spread
To celluloid,
A marble statue
To a living breathing moving image.

She's an exploitation dream,
First lady of Burlesque,
A siren on the screen,
A goddess.
She has the universe
Floating in her hair.
She's here, she's everywhere
And when she dies,
She'll be the Queen of Heaven.

Now the films are gone
And she tours the midwest dives.
The people come to stare
At a famous beauty
In a strip-tease joint.
She illuminates,
She always looks the same,
Time has not been unkind.
She took the step
From celluloid to stage,
A well lit fantasy
To a living breathing former beauty.

She's an exploitation dream,
First lady of Burlesque,
A siren on the screen,
A goddess.
She has the universe
Floating in her hair,
She's here, she's everywhere
And when she dies
She'll be the Queen of Heaven.

Lights low,
Keep the movement slow,
Make-up just a little thick.
Every little tuck and trick
To preserve the illusion
Someone will save her,
Make a record for her,
Then condemn her to
A life of disco.
She took the step
From celluloid to stage
A well lit fantasy
To a living breathing former beauty.

spanish dancing

fuchsia flamenco
1979 london

fuchsia flamenco / half light / tap rhythms / tender fandango of two olive-skinned boys teeth in each other's neck sucking cruel dinner / wide-eyed flamenco dancer her legs around her male partner her arm draped backward / male partner eyes slit, tongue flicking, undulates his head and guides himself into her flamenco dancer, spits as he misguides – snake meets snake on a hot Spanish night / tap rhythms / cheap transistor melts as soft guitar cries from its speaker and flamenco dancer cries at the ruthlessness of her valentino lover fucking out his gypsy frustration / stomach muscles give way / hand flicks open, fan falls to the floor / two broken Spanish dolls / two boys silhouetted / two slender hands grasp the thighs of the flamenco dancer, impaling deeper / tap rhythms, two fushcia scorpions advance, retreat and advance again, circling / flamenco guitar works up to orgasm and cries out as crescendo subsides / scorpions spit poison from raised tails / flamenco dancer glances sideways (must use their choreographer).

She is impaled, his toreador trousers tight
around his backside stabs her olé.
Her claws run down his back
Now they are lost in the dance.
Tap rhythms /
Singer under the window /
Melting transistor radio /
Guitar begins to build up /
Crying woman's voice
bemoaning her cruel treatment /
Sweat on their faces,
Fan flickers with eyes, closes
with eyes to a thin slit /
Fringes from the dancer's split
skirt curls around the curve
of her thigh /
Castanets click with teeth /
Broadway tap rhythms.

marc almond

He bursts from his near-splitting black trousers,
Her tilted adolescent breasts draw him to her,
Sucks a cigarette in a scene she stole
from Carmen Jones.
The two boys have stopped
their love play transfixed
by her swivelling,
Hypnotised by his black eyes.

Skirt raised baring perfect thigh /
Legs taut as heels click /
Cruel motion, darting hand /
Snap fingers, come hither /
Two cobras spit fandango /
Two scorpions fuck in tango /
Drops her fan and throws her hair back /
Wide eyes water and sting with khol black

Snap fingers / click heels / slap
guitar / thrust waist / eyes
welded / knees bended / sharp
gesture / short breath / flicking
tongue / orgasm ended

(she bites his lip)

Two boys fuck in an alley /
Two scorpions dead in a pool of their own poison /
Two cobras, each one's teeth sunk into the other's neck /
Two Spanish dancers in soft sweat focus,
One breaths through limp lips
(doesn't matter which one).

Love you madly

the barriochino

Where the day melts into dusk,
Where the men are bold with
    macho,
And the women gold with musk
Hug the sea that fucks the sand.
The cathedral cries,
The moon expires.
Flamenco drips from glistening
    pores
As whores reach high
And snatch the stars
To braid their pimps as matadors.

The singer's thrust,
Gardenias blush.

Crazies with hash-dusted eyes,
Turbanned, oiled, and clench-
    butted;
Tightrope trip across the squares
Dripping drugs, and flicking drink,
Painted nails
And faggot winged,
Cheer the beggar as she sings.
Heels spear up the dog shit,
Cats cringe as vermin forage,
Pavestones hum, guitars strum
At Bar Darling, Bar La Concha,
Their cock beats upon the belly:
Fountains come.

Rouge on the lips of well-heeled
    cunt.

Striking drain slime,
Fluttering boys,
Sea rot and swollen sun;
Skull-faced moon,
Fishribbed, Gothic noon,
The Barriochino seethes
With dog-knived bitches.
Pint drips from dock blubber,
Cellulite and sucking tongues.
Aniseed, shit-footed, bristles and tit,
Sugar drips into dream poison,
Yellow and wound pus
Bloody bandages, catarrh;
Thick smoky throats,
Thick meat heads of cut dick,
Ripped up, oiled vaginas
And nudging into caved-in thigh,
Hot and prickly, shitty-assed,
Where the days dissolve into sleep,
Where sleep sinks into alleys dark.

In gaudy windows plastic melts;
Transistors scar the view.
Sinister tangoes,
Final cruel jewelled beauty,
Dark beauty:
Eyes of a girl,
Lips of a girl,
Cruel beauty everywhere.

marc almond

The scarred breasts of Brazil,
Ripped bellies of bulls.
Lost limbs
Of the soldiers,
Hacked fingers of thieves,
Twisted spines of cripples,
Raw asses of rent boys,
Tainted lips of whores,
Syphilitic tips of dicks,
Ricketed knees of beggars
Unable to stand:
All in silver, gold, red and lace;
Brushed with fans and seductive
    smiles,
Rich with decay, the acidic sea
Eats the walls and strips the bones.
A galleon heaves in sleep,
Sharks rip Kodaks from
Fat Yankee necks;
Gums suck dick to the roots
And the sun turns arms smack-
    brown,
Opium blushed and touched with
    dew.
The cathedral cries:
The moon expires.
Flamenco drips from glistening
    pores
As whores reach high
To snatch the stars
To braid their pimps as matadors.

bar darling
1987

Where romance meets the real
The ladies bite,
Their perfume stings,
They hustle hard
And fold their muscled arms,
Dreaming of pearls and ruby rings
The old dancer leaves her teeth out,
Makes the table top a stage,
Takes pesetas from the tourists
Who marvel at her age.

The vagabonds play tag,
Use the fountains to get cool,
Steal cameras on the Ramblas,
Run circles round the fools.

Bar Darling
Bar la Concha
Let's love away the drunken hours.
Bar Darling
Bar la Concha
Please be my lady of the flowers.

The moon slips out a-grinning
Where the day melts into dusk,
And the men are bold with masks,
The women sweet with musk.

We douse ourselves in perfume,
Enrich their souls in art,
They may be poor in pocket
But are rich in faith and heart.

And the old singer weaves her song,
I lay thy soul to sleep
Under skies of inky blue
Where angels stop to meet.

Bar Darling
Bar la Concha
Let's love away the drunken hours.
Bar Darling
Bar la Concha
Be my lady of the flowers.

Late afternoon in the Ballenciero
There's a hustle up on the street
Outside the Bar Marseille
Where the thieves and their ladies
    meet.
San Ramón, the street of stares,
Waiting for the saints to unchain
    their hearts;
There the sun never shines in the
    morning
And the afternoon whispers in dark,
Old mothers send their sons on
    their business,
Their faces forever in shade.
The turning of a tarot
And a flicking of a blade:
Mischief waits in the doorway.
His chocolate makes you see stars,
Takes your money and melts into
    shadows
To drink his soul full in the bars.
Down the Ramblas devils are
    waiting
For wallets and jewellery and gold,
Their sinister tangos unload you
And you curse when you find
    you've been rolled.

marc almond

the room below
london 1986

I keep old feelings locked
In the room below;
Soft kisses,
Stained wine glasses,
And outside, the snow.
Broken windows,
Wilting flowers,
And we stayed happy there
For hours.

Oh how I love Carmen Amaya:
She sings my sad
Then happy heart.
How I loved any kind of love,
And you the love of art.

I painted walls flamenco orange,
You painted me
In greys and charcoals.
We stayed together,
Braved the winter:
I was happy
But then I had you.

Oh how I loved Carmen Amaya:
She sings my sad
Then happy heart.
How I loved any kind of love,
And you the love of art.

Sometimes the ceiling would
    collapse,
The upstairs sink leak down our
    walls,
We never washed the cups or dishes;
Well, love can keep you very busy.

Oh how I loved Carmen Amaya:
She sings my sad
Then happy heart.
How I loved any kind of love,
And you the love of art.

lament for banos st sebastian

barcelona 1988

Lament for Banos St Sebastian
Lament for Banos St Sebastian

The muted music from the radio
Seems so alive in my mind,
My heart wants to follow and dance
But I find
I can't.

The heat is wearing her gossamer
    dress,
The day sighs its 'good afternoon',
A bell out at sea
Calling to me:
'Come soon
Come soon'.

'Servicio
Coca Cola
Naranja
Limón',
The man with helados
Is calling the tune
By the side
Of the pool.

The sun on the water
Dances on my eyes,
Endives and olive oil,
A painted sky –
These memories
So deep in me.
Please don't change before I die.
Here I'm sprawled on the stones
In the draining sun
By the pool at Banos St Sebastian
Watching the girls,
The boys, in the water,
Wishing oh wishing
I too had their laughter –
The laughter of youth
And the sparkle of water.

So hazy now
As my heart beats slow,
Things must change
Things must go,
Lament for Banos St Sebastian
Lament for Banos St Sebastian.

marc almond

Flamenco on the radio
And a girl's dusty voice in my mind,
She beckons to follow and dance
But I find
I can't.
She is wearing
A black lace dress,
Her hair in mantillas and braid –
We knelt by the side of the pool,
We knelt
And prayed.

I bend to the water
But find only sand –
Tractors and bulldozers
Have flattened the land.
She smiles and she takes my hand.
Things must change,
Things must go.

I want to call out
But I feel so at peace,
A crumbling façade
Pleading please please release.
And a bell in the distance,
This hot afternoon,
Way out at sea:
'Come soon
Come soon'.

So at peace, so at peace,
Please release, please release.
So at peace, so at peace,
Please release,
Please release.

My hand once in water,
Now buried in sand:
Lament for Banos St Sebastian.

anarcoma

1985
based on a character created by spanish illustrator and cartoonist, nazario

A stiletto scrapes the pavement
Leaving a red streak of paint,
Breaks a sweat upon the sailors
To them she is a saint,
Tattoo on the muscle
That says
'In Love Forever I'.
She'll take them and she'll break
    them,
Oh come hold me till I die

Anarcoma, Anarcoma, Anarcoma

There's a ladder in her nylons
Where we can climb up to the stars,
Join a queue of Borsalinos
As you bend over the bar.
Tattoo on her muscle says
'Beware, Behave, Be Mine'.
She'll eat them up for breakfast,
One at a time.

Anarcoma, Anarcoma, Anarcoma

Well come on if you need loving,
Pirandello don't be shy,
It just takes a little money
And we'll get there by and by,
For I've got a little more
Than any other girl:
You pay a little extra
For a trip around the world.
And if the world is not enough
Then I'll take you to the sky,
Put you in an armhold
Blacken both your eyes.
For you'll find no other woman
That will love you like I do;
I'll just open up the oven door
And leave the cooking up to you.

Anarcoma, Anarcoma, Anarcoma

And she took me to her room
That had never seen the light;
Those sheets had seen a legion
And she beat me up all night,
And over morning coffee
She shook her black hair from its
    mess,
Her lips a gash of lipstick
And she sucks a cigarette.

Anarcoma, Anarcoma, Anarcoma

I could be yours,
You could be mine.
You could be mine.

marc almond

toreador in the rain

1990

Sad little boy of the street,
Hands of a thief
With the mind of a dreamer,
Dodging the puddles with feet
Of a torero in an arena.
Sings an old Andalucian song,
Dancing along
Using his dirty red coat as a cape.

Rain thundering down
Sounds like the applause from
    hundreds of people.
He feels free as the wind,
Free as the swifts around the
    cathedral.
Kneels to acknowledge his fame,
Forgets all his pain,
Little toreador in the rain.

Bathed in a rainbow of pink,
Purple and blue outside El Molino,
The pavement reflecting the neon
Lights this torero in his arena.
He looks down at his clothes
Imagining those
Worn of sequined gold and brocade.

He kneels and kisses the beast,
Fearing the least,
Knowing death will not find him
But maybe one day he will face
The horns of the devil,
His childhood behind him.

Brave young man from the streets,
No more a thief,
No longer a dreamer,
Stands in front of the beast –
A golden torero in an arena.
It starts to thunder and rain,
Remembering that day
He danced like a fool on the wing
    of a dream.

Sand turning to mud,
Soon where his blood will spatter
    and mingle,
Free free as an angel,
Up with the swifts around the
    cathedral,
Never to be seen again.
Dreams all in vain,
There lies the toreador in the rain.

Little toreador in the rain
Little toreador in the rain.

icons of the night and small ad angels

money for love

1992

As the noise of the city dies
The evening has arrived
With so many strange desires.
So many lonely lives:
Cards are placed and ads are taken,
Masks are dropped,
And guilt forsaken.
Names are changed,
Another game began.

Eyes read into other eyes
In busy clubs and bars
And on the street
As darkness falls,
Cars follow cars.

All over telephones are ringing,
Another evening's work beginning,
Meetings are arranged
And deals are done.

Getting money for love

Searching eyes
And lonely faces,
Looking for those soft embraces,
Needing just another moment's understanding.

When you came to the city
You had dreams,
You had plans;
But life is just a vicious circle
Of bills and demands.
You sit upon your single bed,
You clear those problems from your head,
You get yourself all ready
For another night.

Getting money for love

marc almond

l'esqualita

barcelona 1983

Oh I would believe
That she's a real Diva
As she tugs at the reins
Of a hundred chihuahuas.
She'll live a few years
But she'll have some adventures,
Then sing off her sequins
With tears and with traumas.
A fistful of love
With Raoul Kowalski –
He's only a slob of a Corsican
    junkie.
Hoods, Heroin, Hot Janes,
Those fingers of finesse,
Salo aftershave,
Spend the rent on a new dress.

Chi Chi at the bar
Dressed à l'Esqualita,
Talks of Johns and of Joans
And tomorrow's rhinestones.
I'm so sick in my spare time,
Humouring thugs.
We could go out for dinner
But we're always on drugs.

Conchita Piqueur,
She will take on the whole floor,
This Carmen in clingfilm
Will bathe in your applause.
She pads out the glamour
With warmth from your dollars.
Squeeze out your breath
With the strength from her
    shoulders.
OK so it's ham,
But she means every word,
With a ten-minute ballad,
Of despair and blood,

With one hand to the bosom
Paid for by the ballad,
But somewhere in there
Is a deep love for love.

Chi Chi at the Bar
Dressed à l'Esqualita,
Talks of Johns and of Joans
And tomorrow's rhinestones.
Chi Chi at the bar
Dressed à l'Esqualita
Talks of Johns and of Joans
And tomorrow's rhinestones.

I'm so sick in my spare time,
Humouring thugs.
We could go out to dinner
But we're always on drugs.

And somewhere in there
Is a deep love for love
And somewhere in there
Is a deep love for love.

rouge and perfume

for melinda miel

paris 1990

In Paris when I was a girl,
Oh how I loved my youth.
But now behind a layer of paint
I hide a bitter truth.
I used to be a happy girl
And sing a different tune,
But now my life's been tainted by
Rouge and perfume.

I loved a man –
The kind of man
Who fills you with desire.
He took my heart,
I gave it gladly –
Sacrificed to fire.
For he betrayed me,
Made me sad,
Our love would never bloom:
His shirt stained
With another lover's
Rouge and perfume.

And now the mirror shows a face
Of misery and gloom,
A face that hides the sorrow
Painted with rouge and perfume.

He told me I was his first love;
Like honey were his lies,
Sweet were his kisses,
He would have me mesmerised.

The roses that he gave me
Turned to lilies by the moon
To mourn the passing of our love,
Stained with rouge and perfume.

I believed his kisses were exclusive,
I believed his promises divine,
But the stain of violet kisses on his
    silk chemise
Wasn't mine.

I believed he'd never let me down,
I believed he'd love me all the time,
But the cheap and sickly scent
Of violets in his hair
Wasn't mine.
Wasn't mine.

And now you'll find me selling love
On la rue St Denis.
I wouldn't be here
If I'd known
How cruel a man could be.
I lock what's left of my poor heart
Inside a painted tomb
And hide my sadness
With a mask
Of rouge and perfume.

And now the mirror shows a face
Of misery and gloom,
A face that hides the sorrow painted
With rouge and perfume.

marc almond

exotica rose
london 1989

Exotica Rose
Works the shows in the evening;
Exotica Rose
Works for her dollars and dimes;
Exotica Rose,
Nobody knows her secret.
Wherever she goes men shout,
'Hey Rose got the time?'

Exotica Rose,
She dances in beads and in satin,
Tall and bejewelled.
Don't be fooled by her mystery and
    spice :
Her tangos fandangos,
Her grace unmistakably Latin.
You can buy her a drink –
But don't think she's a girl with a
    price.

Exotica Rose
Exotica Rose
Nobody knows
Nobody knows
When she powders her nose
Nobody knows
It's not Exotica Rose.

Exotica Rose
Paints on her face every showtime,
A sequin or two
And a cute shade of blue hides the
    strain.
Two shows a night
But she glows with a glamour
In no time,
She sighs and she shrugs
And she grinds through her routine
    again.
And after her dance
In a dressing room dusty and dirty,
She squints in the mirror
And tells herself never again.
She's pushing an age that hints on
    the wrong side of thirty,
She pulls off her wig
But the stain of the make-up
    remains.

Exotica Rose
Lives in a rented apartment.
She's working all hours
To meet all the bills and demands.
She's a girl with a difference
Or two
In every department:
Life isn't easy
With a wife and two kids on her
    hands.

Exotica Rose
Exotica Rose
Nobody knows
Nobody knows
When she powders her nose
Nobody knows
It's not Exotica Rose.

champagne
new york 1989

A winter morning sun in New York,
Champagne wakes and checks the
    time.
It's hard to keep a cup of coffee
    down
When there's so much on your
    mind,
Kicks a cockroach across the
    bedroom floor,
Checks the mirror grabs some
    clothes,
Waits for the aching to subside
Where to find it no one knows.

And they say you're doing fine
They're just playing with your
    mind,
And they never even know your
    name
But they all want you to shine,
To glitter all the time –
They all want a little taste of
    Champagne.

Takes the subway early afternoon
Downtown to Eighth Avenue
To the Show Palace Theatre
Where Champagne bares all
In a low rent nude revue.
In the darkness shadow people
Stare at Champagne glassy-eyed,
Takes the tips and imitates a smile,
Waits for the aching to subside.

And they say you're doing fine
They're just playing with your
    mind,
And they never even know your
    name
But they all want you to shine,
To glitter all the time –
They all want a little taste of
    Champagne.

Later in a room
On a little glass pipe,
Sweet dreams to help him
Forget his life.

He leans on the wall,
Rolls back his eyes
And says to all the aching goodbye.

Champagne was a dancer I met who worked at the Show Palace Theatre, Eighth Avenue,
New York.

marc almond

the flame

paris 1989
written for marie france

Red light Adonis
Why do you look so blue
When they're all adoring
All adoring you?
Your satin eyes so sinful,
Sad and lonely too,
Glowing like a candle,
Muscled and tattooed.

Lovers fall around you
Like the autumn leaves.
A hard-hearted hero
Laughing as they grieve.
Many have fallen
Where many you deceived,
Bathing in your aura,
Wanting to believe.

The moths are drawn
To the flame
And as they are consumed
You'll learn
Not to go near the flame:
You'll burn
You'll burn
You'll burn.

Lonely men and ladies
All become your toys
For one fleeting moment
They taste your youth and joy.
Red light Adonis
Each night they buy your love,
They only see an angel
Sent from heaven above.

The moths are drawn
To the flame
And as they are consumed
You'll learn
Not to go near the flame:
You'll burn
You'll burn
You'll burn.

And as your light shines brightly,
One day it will expire,
No more fragile hearts
Consumed within your fire.
Only the mirror
Will reveal you as you are:
Burnt out and lovely,
A faded star

Red light Adonis
Why do you look so blue
Are those so adoring
Now ignoring you?
No more friends or lovers,
Only cruel truth,
Nothing dies so quickly
As the flame of youth.

The moths are drawn
To the flame
And as they are consumed
You'll learn
Not to go near the flame:
You'll burn
You'll burn
You'll burn.

the hustler
1986

Over there
In the cold
Stands the hustler,
His eyes are old –
He has seen a million ugly scenes,
Places where men droop with
    mould,
The backrooms
Where soiled goods are sold,
Seen with opened eyes since
Frail fifteen.
He has found it hard at first
But on his brow there sits a curse
For when the young must suffer
At the hands of men.

Memories of Christmas past
Were never there to ever last;
Things as were can never
Be again.

Over there by the wall
Stands the hustler,
He's not very tall,
He's trampled by the jaded, by the
    sly,
He's seen the darker side of men:
First fascinated, and then
He found his urge to laugh,
An urge to cry.

He'll find close friends
No friends at all,
He feels so lonely, tired and small.
How few are chosen from
The golden call.

There's something in us all it seems
To crave adventure,
Hunt for dreams,
But corruption, the seducer, spoils
Our schemes,
And surely as the snow will melt
The hustler
Grabs his soul and heads for home,
With lessons learned under his belt.

Over there
By the wall
Stands the hustler
With the men of law
On either side to flank the sallow
    youth.
But some of us will never learn,
It takes the blow of fists to burn,
How painfully we suffer for the
    truth.

the lonely
go-go dancer

the lonely go-go dancer
london 1996

Lonely go-go dancer
Dancing in crazy foam,
Surrounded by your acolytes
But going home alone.
When did you last see
A sun-drenched afternoon,
When did the morning light
Last invade your room?

Disguise your nightlife pallor
With a tan from a machine,
Behind your ears
A sticky scent
Of decadence and dreams.

They all adore
Your sequined smile,
Revolving in your cloud of blue
Untouchable to anyone,
Anyone but you.

Lonely go-go dancer
On your revolving stage,
Spinning super nova
Of the glamour age.
When did you last feel
The brush of a lover's kiss,
Someone who wants you for you,
Is it love you miss?
As you dance with dreaming eyes,
Sleeping deep,
Your eyes awake,
Thinking of a future
And the money that you'll make.

They all adore
Your sequined smile
Revolving in your cloud of blue,
Untouchable to anyone,
Anyone but you.

Lonely go-go dancer
Wondering to yourself,
Why is one so beautiful
Left upon the shelf?

Who gave you face of angels
Dizzy with aspirations,
Tied you with limitations
To a life of youth and beauty?
Cruel desires
To be a singer,
Fires that burn to be an actor
But with no voice
Or expression
You're trapped in your nightlife
    profession.

Lovely go-go dancer
Give a little
Of your art,
Give your body,
Give your beauty,
But most of all
Your heart.

marc almond

erotic shopping
london 1996

I want the black hair;
I want the blonde;
I like the bizarre
And the demimonde;
I'll take the one with leather and
    lace,
I'll buy the body,
I'll buy the face.

Paper, cash or credit card –
Visa plastic gets me hard
In Earl's Court where the hustlers
    meet
Or New York Forty-second Street.
Let's go erotic shopping
For girls or for boys,
Apparatus and toys.
Let's go
Without stopping;
Whatever we do,
I want to go erotic shopping with
    you.

Spending some cash,
Trading for trash:
I like them cheap,
Straight off the street.
I need a reason
For existing –
Cheap little things,
I'm not resisting.

Let's go erotic shopping
For girls and for boys,
Apparatus and toys.
Let's go
Without stopping;
Whatever we do,
I want to go erotic shopping with
    you.

I tried chocolate,
I tried fashion…
Neither could satisfy my passion.
I don't want it for free –
I've got everything to satisfy me,
I've got everything but a life –
I just need a commodity.

marc almond

porno star

london 1996

Come on to my casting couch
And be my porno star,
Come out of my video –
I've loved you from afar.
How I've played your money shots
On replay and on pause,
Come into my movie house
And bathe in my applause.

You can be
My dream, my icon –
As long as you don't turn the light
    on.
You can burn forever in my
    memory,
You can help to fill the void
Between the glass or celluloid:
You perform to turn me on
And then you're gone.

Come into my satin bed
And look me in the eye,
My electronic cupid
Even after you die.
Come and be my porno star
When night is on my mind,
You turn me on,
I turn you off,
Until another time.

You'll be a love
That never ages;
Only once I pay your wages,
I choose the image.
Kneel before the video –
Your life is making love for others,
You never see your many lovers –
It's all to turn me on
Then I'm gone.

diary of a porno star

Welcome to a tear-stained page
In the diary of a porno star.
We met once over a warm gin and
    lime –
I was stoned and divine,
Somewhere back in my prime.

Did I set free your fantasy,
Did I make your world burn?
Well here I am now –
Your small-ad Messiah –
The five-year-old photo
To kick your desire.
'Is it really you?' you enquire –
No it can't be him,
He was unreal, untouchable.
But now I apply the make-up thick,
Alas I'm just another dick.

In 1996 the porno star has finally crossed over into a more mainstream arena. Cicciolina, Jeff Striker, Aiden Shaw, Tabatha Cash and many others have marketed themslves like pop stars and other icons and celebrities of popular culture – books, videos, t-shirts, records. In America there are yearly awards for the best porno performers, porno stars as models in fashion layouts and on catwalks, porno stars in Broadway plays. These days some people aspire to be porno stars; no longer the exploited nameless and faceless people of past years, the porno star has marketed him- or herself like everything else in the 90s. Sex is a commodity like everything else and it has its own range of consumer goods. I await the day Jeff Striker, Cicciolina or Germany's Dolly Busters presses the button on the lottery show.

marc almond

porno star rising

1996

They deified the porno star,
Put him on a pedestal of sunlight,
Captured him forever
In a picture by Pierre et Gilles.
Still shining,
Like a young god
Of the silver-misted lens:
We remember
When he was just bruised and brutal.

They deified the porn star,
Put him on a TV show at teatime
Giving away prizes and kisses
On the lottery,
Still glowing like Apollo,
In your dreams until tomorrow.
The camera sighed
But stayed above his waistline.

As the TV strips away the magic,
Exposes something tragic
Layers of make-up can't conceal,
Revealing feelings
All too real.
With every move and scripted line
A little mystique dies each time.

Acceptability redeemed you
As they tamed you
And mainstreamed you,
Took away the edge
And dulled your masculinity.
I've lost my imagination –
My satin sheets have turned to nylon.
Let's worship the modern icon
And turn the light on.
Now.

professional friend
london 1996

Does everybody know yet
The circumstances
Under which we met?
I hear the word around
And they're laughing.
Does everybody know yet
The ins and outs
Of our tête-à-tête?
Can they wait
For their next instalment?

Saw you in an ad –
You were made for me –
XXX VWE.
So be my professional friend,
Always reliable to the end –
Always there
To say you care –
How much was that again?

marc almond

they always have a story

london 1992
excerpt from an earl's court story 1

Hey what's your story?
Is it the same as mine?
Is it one of glory
Or one of decline?
But I'm like the waves
Breaking on the shore,
Always back for more.
I'm like the sun –
Always coming out
When there's rain about.
(They always have a story)
Hey what's your excuse?
Is it still the same?
Is it one of abuse,
Or one of gain?
But I'm like the breeze,
Always blowing in
When the storm begins.
But just like the leaves
I fall from the tree
When the storm hits me.

(They always have an excuse)

Well I know someone
Who will see me all right,
I've always got a place
To stay at night.
I've met the famous
And they liked my smile.
I've got a millionaire lover
Who makes it worth my while.

I've money on the way
And luck on my side –
I'll pay you back tomorrow
'Cause I've got my pride.
I've got a job next week
And my friend's an MP –
I know them all
And they know me.
I'm in-between lovers
And I've got no ties,
I'm telling the truth
Just look in my eyes.
I'm like a rock –
I can harden my heart
When things fall apart.
I'm like a ball –
Always bouncing back
When under attack:

That's my story!

kevin's diary
1979

FRIDAY arrived in london 17.00 at victoria station. raining. went to gloucester road wimpy bar to dump my suitcase with a friend who works there. ate a burger. got tube to piccadilly and made my way to the clip-joint booking office. chatted with a man in the seedy surroundings. dim blue light. they have a trick to get money out of the customers, like buying a membership, then extra for the ticket (about £8 altogether). some of the customers get stroppy today. two black gents and some chinese sailors (i think they were chinese) had heated arguments in foreign languages. saw maurice. he was very depressed because he'd lost all his money on a dope deal. asked me to stay with him saturday night but later changed his mind as he wanted to go out with a friend. he was so fed up. went into one of the back rooms in another office round the corner. maurice and his friends were rolling joints. performed favours but they didn't give me any money. i refused one and he got nasty. the place is like a dingy old urinal. a guy from another office took me round the corner. he gave me a couple of quid. he is trying to organise a film for me with the promise of £100. so much ripping off.

SATURDAY stephen dropped me in the west end about 1.00. i made my way to the club in soho. i had arranged to meet maurice and another guy with some clients (£50 a time). nobody turned up. guys working there were cool to me and wouldn't let me in the office. i wandered around town occasionally passing by to see man about the film. he was expecting to hear about it that night. had problems with the guys. performed favours. some for money. jojo was there – a huge fat maltese guy with a top knot like bloody mary from the

marc almond

film *south pacific*. he likes me to flick my tongue at him. he
cries like a baby. i felt sick. this office tonight consists of one
dingy room with flock wallpaper peeling off the walls and
filthy slashed furniture, a disgusting lavatory with no flush
and no sink, only water spouting out of a pipe down the lavatory bowl. here favours are performed. in the room is a table
with soft-core magazines spread out. 'the adventures of big
breasted women'. helped maurice to get the spelling right on
a sign saying 'hard porno films'. made my way to leicester
square to meet stephen. while having a walk down the dilly i
bumped into ginger. i spotted him mincing towards me. he
had just been chatting up a boy he had decided he didn't want
and was now regretting it. we met stephen and took a walk
around the meat rack. it was a real girls' night out with the
effeminate ones out in full force. they stood in little groups
under the arches fluttering their eyelashes, flicking back their
hair and swapping trade stories. rougher boys lean against
the railings, daring anyone to approach them. punters stalk
their prey. they hover around the arches or chat in little
groups, their eyes forever dancing and darting. we spotted
old mother rat bag (the queen mother), 69 yards old and rose,
a friend of ginger's. ginger looks around frantically for the
boy he brushed off earlier. a policeman slides into the scene so
we make off back to leicester square and the self-service café.
i flirt with the chef and he flirts back (i think he's cypriot).
later we walk back to the meat rack but a lot of bargains have
gone for bed and bread, ginger says. some boys look so mean
and they say how butch they are, but as ginger said about one
of these boys who wanted to play queen, 'well, girl, i'd
parked up there for five minutes before i shed my passengers.'

SUNDAY in the evening i made my way to the dilly and the bali hai office to see maurice. this is another office where clients book for films or a live show. they pay their money (as much as you can get out of them). then they are taken round the corner to see the film or show. the office is up a darkish alley and has a string of coloured light bulbs outside (only half of them working) and a few soft-core tit mags inside. we try to call the customers in and once or twice nearly succeed, but it is a dead night, as quiet as the grave. a girl comes in to sell some photos of herself. maurice takes her around the corner to see a prospective buyer. i am left alone to look after the shop. i feel scared, any lunatic could come in and i'm on my own. i was relieved when maurice came back. i had sent a punter round the corner as i didn't know exactly how much to charge him. maurice cursed me and sent me running after the punter, telling me to charge him anything he'd pay. i caught up with him but he said he was too pissed and didn't want to know.

but i'm alive

I'm a survivor
Who never asks why;
Use or be used
Is the motto I live by.
I still have a heart
But I lock it deep inside,
Or put it on a shelf
Along with my pride.

I've heard all your promises,
Your plans or your schemes,
But I've had too many people
Walking over my dreams.
Life's a lonely drag –
But I'm alive.

From the Earl's Court Road
To the West End lights,
I walked my tears away
Night after night.
I've envied lovers
And the family tie,
But I know no other way
But leave them and lie.

Too late to collect
All the favours that I'm owed,
So I'm hitching a ride
Down purgatory road.
Life's a lonely drag –
But I'm alive.

Film directors tell me
My face is a winner.
Record company scouts
Say I could be a singer.
I've read all the scripts
But I'm inside their heads:
There's an easy route to stardom
And it leads to their beds.

I've seen all my options
Going straight up the river –
They go up in smoke
When I fail to deliver.
Life's a lonely drag –
But I'm alive.

I know all the scams –
The stings and the schemes –
I've still got my hopes,
I've still got my dreams.
I still keep my smile
In what I go through –
There's always someone worse off
    than you.

I'm alive;
At least I'm alive.

I've still got my hopes
I've still got my dreams
Hold on to your pride
For whatever you do
There'll always be someone
Worse off than you

London 1992

dog with three legs

excerpt from an earl's court story III

You're a narcoleptic angel,
An innocent abroad,
Still falling for a promise
As you hang on every word.
Sometimes you shine with worldly
   knowing
Like a child of second sight,
I need some of your knowledge
So come and stay the night.
You can be my plank of wood,
You bruised young thing,
You sleepy head,
Roll over and play dead –
My dog with three legs.

Your broken nose
Is like a wounded bird
I want to cherish to flight.
You've got your story –
I've got mine –
So come and stay the night.

You can be my plank of wood,
You bruised young thing,
You sleepy head,
Roll over and play dead –
My dog with three legs.

You wake as I am sleeping,
Troubled by the moon,
Where there was a puppy
A wolf will wake up soon.
Darkness in your blue eyes
To cloud your second sight,
Soon I'll be regretting
You came to stay the night.

I'll be still like a plank of wood,
A bruised white face,
A bleeding head,
I roll over stone cold dead
For my dog with three legs.

marc almond

the muscle boy

the taiwan bar cabaret

1991

I wake each afternoon,
Look around my little room.
I play some music,
Take a shower,
And try to kill each lonely hour.

At seven o'clock
Each night I go
To bar Taiwan
To do a show.
The customers,
They like to see
A muscle show performed by me.
To many customers I sell
My time, my smile, my body as
    well.
These are all for sale
But you can see
A number where my heart should
    be.

With the little money
That I make
I buy some shoes,
A shirt or two.
I pay my rent
And eat enough
To keep my strength,
To see me through.

Every morning before dark
I work out at Lumpini Park.
Admirers sit and look at me:
I give them a good show for free.
So many say 'I love you'
But may stay an hour and go.
One hour or two a promise,
But by now I should know
They only love the surface
And in time they'll soon be gone –
I know I've only one heart
So I save it for the one.

the lady boy

taiwan bar cabaret

1991

Lady Boy
With your lipstick and fan,
Dancing the light fantastic.
Lady Boy
Finding love where you can,
Playing with your beads of plastic.

You've got to dance,
Dance your tears away.
No one can say
That you can't take it.
Dance until the light of day,
Dream of a way to make your fame,
Lady Boy.

Lady Boy
With your tough attitude –
Devil may care
What you wear tomorrow.
Crazy boy,
All the guts in the world
To cover what you feel of sorrow.

You've got to dance,
Dance your tears away.
No one can say
That you can't take it.
Dance until the light of day,
Dream of a way to make your fame,
Lady Boy.
Lady Boy,
Hold your microphone high
And mime to the diva's sorrow.
Lady Boy,
Glitter on your eyes,
You're going to be a star tomorrow.

In this life
You gotta fight for the right
To be what you want to be,
Do what you want to do.
In this life
You gotta take what you can,
Or someone will take it from you.

big dick show
taiwan bar cabaret III
1991

The music stops,
The lights dim low –
Meet Bo –
Who proudly presents
His big dick show.

In a pink fluorescent light
And a touch of smoke,
Bo poses athletically, artistically,
Dick upright,
To the front, to the left,
The north, the south,
The tourist with the open mouth
And it's true it shows a lot.

And proud he is right to be,
For no rarer a sight
Than a big dick in Bangkok.

beautiful twisted night

madame gin sling sings

taiwan bar cabaret IV

1991

All silent now
For the mistress of
The house of flesh,
The Chinese dragon
In her nest.

As Madame Gin Sling sings,
The music a little melancholic,
Tongued with a mystery exotic.
Tears through her
Blank heart like a tornado,
Ripping up the dead roots,
All burnt wood.
With a fearsome torch,
She scorches
Those who dare
To stare in awe.

She always gives much more
Than she ought to,
And those who gaze, adore
When Madame Gin Sling sings.

She brings up the poison,
The bitterness
That love has bought her.
She scorches us
With her sweat and tears,
In each diamond drop
A perfectly formed core of hatred
And just a little lust

Her face a pock-marked mask
Of make-up and madness,
A Noh nightmare,
An apocalyptic vision
In cobra-black sequins,
With needles in her hair –
Medusa with her dead-eye stare.

Slicing off hair with her fan,
Part gorgon, part man,
Part courtesan.
Go-go boys
And lady boys,
Wax dancers
Sit at her feet in homage.
And oily muscle boys
Take the strain
And try to smile
As she swoons in dead faint
In their arms.

A miasma of salaciousness and
    desire
Of evil and torment and torture.
Heartache
Plus jaded capriciousness,
Sweet and sour deliciousness.
Evaded beauty
And paralysed yawn,
Once again is calm.

And all felt the fear that brings
When Madame Gin Sling sings.

marc almond

for only you

london 1996

And as the sun goes down
I wait for you to call,
Sometimes I wait in vain
For you don't come at all.
Am I just one of
Many others that you see?
Are they beautiful and fun,
More desirable than me?
I sell myself to men
But then it's never love –
I give them smiles and empty words,
No more than enough.

Sometimes you bring some wine,
Sometimes you bring a flower –
It's special even though
You only stay an hour.
My body is for loan
So what else can I do
But save my love for one,
The one and only you?

Sometimes it may be days,
Sometimes it may be weeks,
Before I stroke your hair,
Before I kiss your cheeks.
Some others want my love –
I always tell them no –
They do what men must do,
And then they go.
Some want to make me rich,
Some always want to give –
I tell them I just need enough to eat,
Enough to live.

Sometimes you bring some wine,
Sometimes you bring a flower –
It's special even though
You only stay an hour.
My body is for loan
For what else can I do
But save my love for one,
The one and only you?

I wonder if you know,
Though I do what I do,
I cry each time you go,
Each time the hour is through.
I'm dreaming of a time
That you will think of me
As more than
Just a lover paid in full.

And as the neon floods
My tiny room each night,
I think of years ahead
And of my lonely life.
At least I had a love –
Though that love was small –
Better to have loved and lost
Than never to have loved at all.
One day you'll say goodbye
And you'll not return,
Never knowing of the fire
In my heart that burns.

Sometimes you bring some wine,
Sometimes you bring a flower –
It's special even though
You only stay an hour.
My body is for loan
So what else can I do
But save my love for one,
The one and only you?

hell

germany 1996

When I first met you
You were in a mess,
Lying in a pool of hopelessness,
Eyes full of lies
And a head full of blind ambition.

Coy little tart
With your cheap love bites,
Head full of lycra
And Saturday nights,
Easy to break
When your heart's set on
    demolition.

You learned your trade
Around eleven,
South of sugar-daddy heaven.
Girl, you made the rent,
You made them sing.

I stood watching you dance,
Working the room,
Intoxicating
Like a sleazy perfume.
You're Satan as an angel,
I know your game so well –
Your promise is of paradise
But your love is hell.

On our second meeting
You'd climbed a little more
Up the crooked ladder
From the bedroom floor,
Old for your years
But fresh with your inspirations.

Streetwise little schemer
With your cutoffs and slap,
Different little story
Everytime you came back,
Smelling of cheap hotel soap
And desperation.

You found a niche
In being a party
For the homo glitterati.
Lolita on your tongue,
They loved you young.

I stood watching you dance,
Working the room,
Intoxicating
Like a sleazy perfume.
You're Satan as an angel,
I know your game so well –
Your promise of paradise
But your love is hell.

marc almond

Remember way back to a time
Of cheap eyeliner, five and nine?
A child, your eyes in a pencil black,
No easy route, no turning back.
Dyed your hair jet black or blonde,
Of blue mascara you were fond.
Spinning in the nightclub light,
Blue rivers down your cheeks each
    night.
Cheep alcohol and glitterdust
Made northern boys go blind with
    lust.
Based your life on female stars,
Risked your life in strangers' cars,
You clicked your heels along the
    path of life.

On our third and final meeting
You'd become a local star:
They've all had you at the disco,
In the bathroom or the bar.
Always borrowing some money,
Trying to chase a better euphoria.

Honest in your treachery,
Truthful to your fame –
One moment lighting up the world,
The next you're gone again.
Soon your legend faded
And we were to see no more of you.

Some say you've gone to New York
And others say you're ill –
I'm just sending you a message
That I'm thinking of you still.

I stood watching you dance,
Working the room,
Intoxicating
Like a sleazy perfume.
You're Satan as an angel,
I know your game so well –
Your promise of paradise
But your love is hell.

Hell

Hell

beautiful twisted night

antonio

naples 1985

She combs her hair in the morning.
She kisses me and sighs my name.
She turns to me and without warning,
Pays me for our little game.

She keeps me tied to her, a prisoner
With this chain of gold around my neck,
And the diamond watch that ticks away the
    hours
Handcuffed to my wrist lest I forget.

That I am at her beck and call each evening,
A Brylcreem genie to grant every wish,
A stud to quench unsatiable desires,
A taste of youth served on a silver dish.

Her friends all talk of me in lowered voices –
They say 'the lights are on but no one's home' –
But they give me a pat upon the backside
And the number of their telephone,
And in-between the sheets they say they love me,
The hottest lover they've ever had,
And as they reach into their Gucci handbags
I feel a little empty, little sad.

Each look into the cruel mirror
Shows me a new wrinkle every day –
For a life of luxury and pleasure
There comes a time the piper I must pay.
And with each birthday comes a sinking feeling –
Last year as my age reached twenty-five –
Who'll want a latin lover reaching thirty?
Who'll give a damn that I'm even alive?

marc almond

None of these wealthy ladies want to marry,
They see me as a trinket and a toy,
They say there's nothing going on above the
    waistline –
It's not my brain they're wanting to employ.
And bitterness will set in like a cancer,
Lines around the mouth, around the eyes –
I'll tell them I am still within my twenties.

One more addition to a life of lies.

And suddenly the telephone stops ringing,
No more old ladies coming on to me
And the spread of middle age is bringing
Realisation and responsibilities.
I'll find a nice young girl and maybe marry,
Someone who'll love me for the man I am,
Not a gigolo who makes love for the money –
For deep inside there waits a loving man

Milan
Naples
Florence
Rome
If you're a lady and alone,
Just pick up the telephone,
And call Antonio.

Antonio!

jamie dream

1995

Jamie was a runaway,
Life was full of pain,
He was just sixteen,
Jamie left with nothing but his
    dreams.

His motorbike
By the side of the road,
They all thought he'd died
Or a suicide,
But Jamie headed
For the London scene.

In Jamie shone a light
Of neon and of night,
A mind so full of stars
To block out teenage scars.
Jamie Jamie Jamie Dream,
Standing by the fruit machine,
How does it feel to be
King of the scene?
And how does it feel to be free
Jamie Dream?

Jamie tried to lose himself,
Getting out of his head,
Looking for an escape,
Grabbed at chances,
Didn't hesitate.
Bruised on the violent street,
Jamie learned to survive,
Tried to stay alive.
But Jamie sometimes
Felt his heart would break.

But Jamie learned the rules –
Losing was for fools –
Life always on a bet,
A big game of roulette.

Jamie Jamie Jamie Dream,
Standing by the fruit machine,
How does it feel to be king of the
    scene
And how does it feel to be free?

Soon everybody knew his fate,
Charmed by his streetwise style;
And those that thought they'd lost
    him
Would soon be reconciled.
You'd feel the world was on you
And Jamie would make you smile:
Jamie knew he could get what he
    wanted
By just being Jamie

Jamie now just twenty-two
But wise in his head
From what he's been through.
He's still not sure quite what he
    wants to do:
Jamie still has heartache inside
But he's learned to survive
And he's tough on his pride.
He knows that life's
Just something you hold on to for
    the ride,

And a trail of broken hearts
Will show you where he's been,
From those who only dream of
    Jamie Dream,
Jamie Jamie Jamie Dream ...

marc almond

trials of eyeliner

Trials of eyeliner,
Styles of eyeliner,
Eyeliner saved your life –
Playing up the vamp
You were applying mystery,
Setting yourself free.
Free.

Bitten nails down to the quick,
Black nail varnish painted thick,
You were a tortured martyr, Saint
    Divine
For ugly boys who want to shine.
Father viewed your eyes of black,
Responded with a violent slap,
Said you made him feel ashamed:
'Get out and don't come back.'

Went to Soho,
Worked the clips,
Met Chinese sailors on
Leave from their ships.
Mascara gave you deep allure
Of your sex.
They couldn't be sure –
They were falling in love
With you falling in love with
    yourself,
And in the light of the basement
They didn't care enough.

Took a trip to New York town,
Leather boys all round,
Tried to get into their club,
Doorman gave you quite a snub:
Pointed to the sign above the door –
Only denim and leather to be worn –
'Too much black eyeliner, dear
Not a chance of coming in here.'

Trials of eyeliner,
Styles of eyeliner,
Eyeliner saved your life –
Playing up the vamp
You were applying mystery,
Setting yourself free.
Free.

love to die for

new york 1994

How sweet and dark is love
When you have the taste for blood.

Fantasy dancer,
Dangerous rhythm,
Dance me your dance
Of love forbidden.

It's love to die for,
Love to cry for,
Love to say goodbye for.

Dance your way into my heart
Where I can love your scars,
They tell me what you like,
They tell me who you are.
Come on and take my hand –
You'll soon be seeing stars –
And when you dance I dream
Of love in the extreme.

Paint your eyes
In thrill vermillion;
Pout your lips,
Bare your teeth,
And look ferocious.
You're to die for,
You're to cry for,
You're to say goodbye for.

So what's on the menu –
Is it violence again?
And is that blood or lipstick
With which you're writing your
    name?

You cut deep with sorrow,
You carve it with disdain,
And when I get you home
You'll never be alone again.

Violence
Violence
Violence
The violence of your love
Violence
The glamour of your violence
Violence
The violence of your love.

marc almond

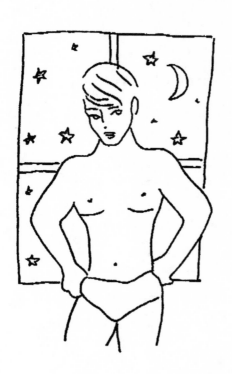

boys in the burger king
1985

The puddles trap the reds and blues,
Sweet neons of the night
Wash the grey of rainy days,
Burning from the light.
The boys sleep in the Burger King,
Elbows in the ash,
And dream of tubes of UHU glue
And plastic bags of trash.

kicked
1985

His face is a pock-marked
Pin cushion, punched-out pool
Of a million lies.
Sneer on the lips
And smear on the smile,
A history of insanity in his eyes.
Eight inches of steel,
Nine inches of flesh,
Doesn't care where he sticks the tip.
Had so many kickings
It's become second nature
And now he gets a kick from the kick.

the club
1992

Come on down to the club
Where the dead are standing up,
You can make love to a mystery boy
Underneath the stairs.
We can trip out on our favourite drug,
We can slip out of consciousness.
I can kiss your paralysed face
And crack up.

marc almond

mr midnight sun

1994

Mr Midnight Sun,
Gold teeth and guns,
You're the Nero of need,
The crown Prince of bleed.
You've gotta run
Until the daylight catches up.
Ease up my heartache
With your solid silver dream –
Can't you hear me screaming
    midnight?
Come on come on.

What goes on,
Mr Midnight?

Mr Midnight Sun,
Bright as your gun,
Supplying the need
Of neon and speed.
You've gotta move
Until the daylight catches up.

Shine your translucent light,
Take away my tears tonight.
You can hear me crying,
Midnight come on come on.

What goes on,
Mr Midnight?

Black Cadillac
Tanked up on crack,
Wired on the lead
Of neon and speed.
You gotta go out in a
Big blaze of glory on the run,
Just a chocolate gangster
Melting in the morning sun.
Guns are drawn at midnight
We shout, come on come on.

What goes on,
Mr Midnight?

dad's little secret

london 1995

Something lurks behind the closet –
Something dirty and obscene –
Something worn with sticky pages,
Something only dad has seen.

Dad has fantasies of bondage,
He has fantasies of rape
But he keeps them to himself,
To himself to masturbate.

When he sits down
With his family
For his breakfast, for his tea
A little darkness
Dad suppresses,
Doesn't want them all to see.
Dad is still a normal dad,
As normal as you and me –
Loves his wife
Loves his children –
Dotes upon on his family.

Mother doesn't know the secret
Fantasies her husband hides,
Doesn't know him well at all
That's why he'd never confide.

Dad he likes to visit Soho;
Sees a model once a week,
Makes him sit still in a corner,
Gags him so he can't speak.
Dad loves seamed and silken
    stockings,
Dad loves soft and golden hair,
Golden hair of finest nylon
Of the type that dad can wear.

Sometimes he likes to watch a
    movie
Of the undercover type,
Helps release a little tension,
Helps him make it through the
    night.

tears, trash and decay

angels
los angeles 1981

The car drives on
Through suburbia,
Ever after.
This is the last game of all,
After this is a down, down slide
And I think I may
Disappear.
This is where reality ends
And the rest takes over
(And it's taking over here).

Running wild
In a sulphate-smeared nightmare,
Scorpio rising,
Houses forever,
And the fantasy's bigger and better.

I've never liked a fantasy that I
    couldn't beat,
And the message goes:
Love me or else,
Because I may die tomorrow
And that may prey
On your minds forever.

The zombie bars,
The big black cars,
And playing the part
Of disposable stars.

The sun is burning my shoulder
And the city it stretches
Away on a plain,
And wow!
I'm feeling like God again.

Or sucking the smoke
In a Greek café,
Wincing at the taste
Of the Turkish tea.

Avoiding eyes
Telling lies,
The things that make me happy –
There is always the distance, the
    dancing
And the black, black heat –
And the stubble breaking through
The TV make-up
(The orange industrial kind),
Which is starting by now
To look a little tainted.

Or the West Side,
The other world
Where the wind
Whistles throught the meat hooks
And the laying with danger,
Like running your tongue
Down a knife-edge.

marc almond

This character is getting boring
    now:
Time to look
For another game.

It was the silence
On the phone
And the last look you gave me was
    cold.
It was the silence
On the phone
And the last look you gave me was
    cold.

You bastard!
This last look you gave me was
    cold.

You said,
You bastard!
This last look you gave me was
    cold.

And the car drives on
Through suburbia ever after,
This is the last game of all
This is the last game of all
Of all!

tarnished

I'm watching you stare mystified
As your silver turns to gold,
But all things tarnish
In the end,
The process we call growing old.
Love the little chipped red nails,
The yellow round the quick,
The little lines
And sinking signs
As you let the beauty slip.
Never mind the grit, the grime,
Mascara clogs the lashes,
Some things only improve with age –
What once was beauty, still is.

I'm out on another date with despair
And I'm paying the bill once more.
I'm just out for a quick kill
The expense is no barrier – who cares?
You don't want my heart anymore.
Drinking and slithering
Under the table,
Cheap eyeliner burning my eyes,
Crawling after that feeling
You slipped in my drink,
In the glass that I threw on the floor.
The insults we sprayed,
Cruelty games that we played,
Getting no further nowhere.
Words forming
On lips that are loosened with drink,
Don't know what they're saying them for.
Queasy queer with Tequila
That rolls in my stomach,
If only I'd cut my own throat.
My fingers reach blindly for one of your
    cigarettes,
Forgetting I don't even smoke.

marc almond

my heart in my shoes

london 1984

Holding my nose for thirteen floors,
The lift is a toilet
Without any door.
Underneath me
The stains
Of the piss and the ash,
It clogs into mud
With the human trash.
Gasp for a breath
In the soft of my shirt,
A sanctuary
From the poisonous dirt.

Every beauty spot
Starts to look like another –
It's the back rooms
And the bar rooms
That really matter.
Cruelty is the human
And kindness the dumb,
You learn this lesson of life
When you're under the thumb,
Crushed under heel
Like a cigarette stub,
What sticks in your mind
Is the loud lack of love.
Sitting alone
You want to give it all up,
Resign yourself smiling
To the fact that life sucks.

Feel the sweet breeze of freedom
On the spaghetti western plains,
A slim black horse
To take me away,
Maybe a place where it's always
    spring
And knee-deep in romance.
It's my heart in my shoes
That's making me dance

But knee-deep in romance
Is knee-deep in pollution –
The thrown-away, blown-away
Present a solution
To my eyes getting tired
With this fresh air and colour:
Give me peeling of paint
And the glamour of squalor.

Every beauty spot
Starts to look like another
It's the back rooms
And the bar rooms
That really matter.
Cruelty is the human
And kindness the dumb,
You learn this lesson of life
When you're under the thumb,
Crushed under heel
Like a cigarette stub,
What sticks in your mind
Is the loud lack of love.
Sitting alone
You want to give it all up,
Resign yourself smiling
To the fact that life sucks.

my former self
1982

Remember me?
I was the boy
With the angel's eyes
And the blush in surprise
When you held my
Hand in full view.
Now I'm so wrecked
That my eyes bleed.
Watch me recede,
Nails curl back from the quick
As they curl with my lip,
Standing limp
In the pool of the light
So callous and cruel,
Bones are piercing me through
And a shadow of you
Meets the shadow of my
Former self.
A quick recollection
And smile
For old times.
Sometimes I feel
That I'm being unkind.
Skin tight
Yet sallow
Saddened by the shallow,
Reaching for the glow,
At the end of the tunnel.
Somewhere up the ladder stands I,
Slumped as the car
Drives over the curb to the wall
And the hiss of the steam
Is the siren
Calling me on to the rocks,
Always as ever
In no man's land,
With my driver
Slumped over
My wheel.

marc almond

once was

Dancing,
The little lights are dancing
And the clock on the wall
Is announcing
Another day.
I keep hearing things
You used to say.
Go away.

And your mouth so dry
As you fake the kiss,
Playing the part
The best you can,
Lying there naked across the sheets
Like a lizard in the sun,
Beckoning me
And failing to see
The little girl you've become.

And you fall,
As you slink
Across the room,
Your lips parted
In a kiss,
Parading your flesh
In the way you know best,
Like a broken seductress.

And I'm casting my mind back
To my fourteenth year
When I learned about
What we call
The pleasure of love;
And it was new to me, then,
And a wave of sadness
Shivers my skin
As I think about
What will never
Be felt again.

galina dances

st petersburg 1992

City of decaying dreams,
Where under a pink sky,
Gold spires gleam,
Glitter like
A dying fire,
Daring angels to fly higher,
Where the Czar
Took a trip,
Hallucinogenic sinking ship
Of sad canals
And endless streets,
Dark canyons
Where young lovers meet.

Galina dances
Under red stars,
Throwing kisses to the dead Czars,
And the soldiers do their duty
In the thighs of sleeping beauty.

City of a million souls
Keep afloat the city –
A million men that died
To keep her pretty.
A wedding cake
Slowly decaying,
As the Russian band is playing.
The dancer swirls
In her torn dresses,
A sleeping angel now confesses
Sins of dead princesses.
This is where the powers of the
    world meet,
Where we kneel at an icon's feet.

Galina dances
Under red stars,
Blowing kisses to the dead Czars,
And the soldiers do their duty
In the thighs of sleeping beauty.

Beautiful decaying city,
Boys and girls so proud, so pretty,
Dancing in their vodka dreams,
Nothing is quite as it seems.

'Galina Dances' was inspired by my visit to St Petersburg in 1992 on my acoustic tour of Russia and Siberia. My visit to Russia is almost a book in itself. St Petersburg is one of the most beautiful places I've ever visited. Galina is Galina Brezhnev, the daughter of the old Soviet president

marc almond

the old arcade

london 1984

Blacked eyes
And swollen angel hips,
Now slumped against
The fruit machine.

A lonely-hearted
Broken Prince,
Calling down the ghosts from limbo
In the dusty old arcade.

I found you
Among the broken pinball tabs,
Shattered one-arm jacks,
And I slipped underfoot on tears
Of a hundred years.
How lonely souls
Gather here for warmth
Making plans to haunt me.
Nowhere so tragic
As a resort out of favour,
Beaches awash with waste
Whispers from summer in love.
But now I stand alone
Weeping in the old arcade
And I think of you.

Beware those blue-jeaned
    Casanovas
With their cut-throat pallors,
Cut-throat, cut-price,
And cut down to size.
The old deckchair man
With a green sea sweat
And broken-down muscle.
Storm-choked,
Tear-soaked,
Lover of a million smiles
And ghost of a million miles.

I am lonely
And my heart is like the old arcade
Somewhere down the promenade,
Choked with sand,
I pushed a penny in the fortune
    teller's hand.

I watched fireballs falling into the
    sea,
Just you and me
And my lifeline, the tide line,
A key to my heart.
My life is forever searching,
My heart forever hurting –
Take me to the brink of another
    threshold
Of pain, of love in limbo.

beautiful twisted night

slave to this

new york 1983

Fear threat and filth,
Tender in hate,
Slug and stab,
Trap and take.
Another trap:
Meat rack and ruin,
Boarded up,
Beaten up.
Gangs roaming the street
Have no respect for a life,
A limb,
A love –
Whose love are you anyway?
Mother smiles,
Narrow eyes,
'Drink up your poison
Like a good little girl –
Can't have your coke
And beat it you know.'

'Sick of seeing you boozed up, burnt
    out
Ugly and low'.
So sick and tired
Of being sick and tired,
Of being used and abused,
That's right.

Pushing through the pavement
    sprawl
Round the late-night supermarket,
Dirtlocked lady
Who hits you in the chest
When you don't want to give her
    money;
Mr Barefoot all the year round,
Please don't breathe on me;
Oh and hi there
Zizi Jean (night)mare.

Still sticky from you,
Still sticky from me.
Smack 'kerpow'
Into the cold Greaseburger Prince.
Call me
Chico from Puerto Rico.

Guilty of
Another cold-handed sperm murder
Forever the crunch of make-up
    underfoot.

Where will you take me
When this is all over?
Somewhere I don't have to
Shiver in the shadows.
So sick and tired
Of being used and abused.

marc almond

Everyday
You get up,
Go to work
Floating like the ash
In the Coffee Pot Café,
Throwing up on an over-diet
Of slob culture.
Scared for you,
For me.
I got so tired of
Reading about
'The anguish of being'
That I ended up being
without.
And where will you take me?
Away from this hell to be
(or not to be).
Pull up the vacancy sign in your
    eyes –
I've seen it and I don't like it.

Only God may find a way
Where there is no way;
That's right.
Is this the last night in Sodom?
That's right.

love among the ruined

So OK you think I'm some kind of
Semolina-headed,
Fired and fettered
Little virgin.
Well, that's OK with me.
One arm in the ashtray,
One arm round your neck
Pulling you across the six-week sheets
    to me.
Oh! You see,
I could be a walking one-man career
For some psychiatrist.
It's true,
I'm open to everyone,
Unique to few.
What about you?
Yeah! What about you?
A sleaze burger,
Grease grimer,
Eyeliner, Whiner:
Up to your ears in a mecca of broken
    dreams.
Only just getting by
With another calculated lie.
Your lobotomy eyes
Tell me a million different versions
Of what you've been
And what you've seen,
Trying to dodge the shadows
Of the lights upon the tarmac.
Desperation kicks me to the kill.
But baby!
I'm waiting at the station
For my train to ruination,
Trying to find a way to cheat the bill.
If they hit you one cheek
Then smash them on the other,
It's a knuckle-duster path
We walk to survive.

Pinch myself and shake the sand out
    the seams,
Until the time
To climb out of the litter bin arrives.
Loose-limbed and lycra-lipped,
My lipsalve sticks on you,
Blitzed and bomber-bug eyes.
Bite the soft skin on the inside;
Resist the watering sensation
To bite my way right through.
All washed up and nowhere to go
All washed up and nowhere to go
Nowhere to go,
To go.
The kitchen smell,
All burnt and smoked up,
Soaked-up stale milk,
Rotten peel across the floor.
Watch you with admiration
As you get yourself together,
To peel the damp dried
Teabags off the wall,
Salvage up some sugar
To sweeten up together,
From the bugs that bite,
Escaping from the bed.
Love this riddled ruin.
Be the bag to hide my head in,
Or walk the weary way
To desolation day, instead.
We're waiting at the station
For our train to ruination,
Who cares the destination!
Who cares if we arrive!
The smell of us,
The damp
That eats the bathroom round the tile
Something tells me
We've been here all the time.

marc almond

death

first time

london 1982

Looking down into your acid eyes
I see a thousand wild nights,
Rubbing your hand in the softest way
Across your necklace of bites.
The streets are deserted
And so is your mind,
We're so sick of the sight of each other –
We've done this many times

Remember way back when
You were so shy and naïve?
Remember the day you lost your youth upon
    the beach?
And a demon killed an angel
As you came over the bed.
So this is the big deal,
The ultimate feeling,
They claim in those books you read.

The feeling of skin against skin
As you feel you slide inside
And you shut your eyes in a wild relief
As you watch innocence die,
As you watch innocence die.

Looking down into your acid eyes
I see a thousand wild nights,
Rubbing our hand in the softest way
Across your necklace of bites.
The streets are deserted
And so is your mind,
Wondering why we never can relive
Our very first time,
Our very first time.

marc almond

stories of johnny

london 1984

Try hard to make the world look bright today,
Try hard to make my nightmares go away,
Try hard to keep the fear away, the cold of day, try hard.
Try hard to play the games the world would like you to play.

But people, they don't really listen,
Their smiles are the keys to the prison.
I'll call on the angels to hold my head softly,
They'll always remember ... stories of Johnny.

Try hard to make my anger go away,
Try hard to make my money last the day (no way),
Try hard to keep away the pain, stop the rain, try hard.
Try hard to fly a thousand miles away.

But people, they don't really listen,
Their smiles are the keys to the prison.
I'll call on the angels to hold my head softly,
They'll always remember ... stories of Johnny.

But people, they don't really listen,
Their smiles are the keys to the prison.
I'll call on the angels to hold my head softly,
They'll always remember ... stories of Johnny.

My smokey lover – will close my eyes forever ... stories of
Johnny.

the gondolier

venice 1990

Oh Mr Gondolier
I need some time to rest,
Please take me on a journey to the
   stars.
At this hour of the day
Only you can take the pain away,
If you're who I think you are.
Though you seem to be smiling,
It's very hard to tell ,
And your singing
Could be the ringing of the old
   cathedral bell.
And your boat is decorated
With the colours I know so well:
They remind me of the colours of a
   funeral.

Through decaying streets we float,
Your boat a ghostly vessel
For an old forgotten heart.
The passageways where Casanova
Played his games of love,
Now haunted and dark.
Deception permeates
The vicious cracks that climb the
   wall,
Like the darkness in my soul.
I recognise it all,
Like the old Venetian glory
I'm ready for a fall,
And I can't see my future.
Mr Gondolier,
From the balconies and balustrades
Young lovers in each others' arms
Enjoy the evening sun,
Throwing flowers from the bridges,
So free from bitterness,
A hundred years away
From what I've become.
But those flowers
Are the golden hours,
The dreams I threw away.
I want to call and warn them
There's so much I want to say;
And that like this sinking city
My heart's rotten with decay,
But I can't find my voice
Mr Gondolier.

I trail my fragile hand
In the murky water,
Dredging up the laughter from the
    past,
A phantom of regret
Dancing in reflected light,
Those blissful nights
I prayed would last.
And silently we glide
Underneath the Bridge of Sighs.
I forget about tomorrow
As I slowly close my eyes
And maybe it's the sun,
Or perhaps I'm going blind.
But I can't see your face,
Mr Gondolier.

My life is growing dark,
Sleep invades my mind with dreams
And tricks of the light.
I see two gates before me
Decorated with symbols of the
    night,
I see all my life before me spinning
As they slowly part,
Remorse it overcomes me
For the evil in my heart.
And suddenly I feel afraid,
It's growing very dark.
I turn,
You've disappeared,
Mr Gondolier
Mr Gondolier …

she took my soul in istanbul

london 1988

Once in a night
I spent in Istanbul
I had a dream of a forbidden world
Where even angels fear
To look upon;
A place where all of love is doomed
    to die.

Her face appeared
Through clouds of bitter wine,
Sour as the morning's early hours.
She took my hair
And she curled it round her fingers.
I was but a fool for love.

The scent of Turkish oils
Mixed with the harsh tobacco
In the overcrowded bar;
Hashish
And cool mint in her hair.
I was a fool for love,
I was a fool.

She sang to me
A torch song softly laced
With mysteries Arabian:
It poisoned my mind,
A sickness in my soul.
I tried,
I didn't want to hear at all.
A curtain fell
Before my eyes, I did
Succumb into her healing breast.
She sang that song,
I gave her all my soul,
And my all
To the pleasure of the flesh.

I cried that night
For those forsaken times,
Those times when I was
Simply satisfied.
I turned to dust
That night a thousand times,
That night a thousand times I died
    inside
And through what's left
Of my sad life I hear
Her singing in the fevers of the
    night.

HER
Look into the mirror of my eyes
And tell me what you see:
It's not your love I need.
You'll see
Sorrow, tears and darkness,
These are the pleasures
Beyond your dreams.

I found myself
Down by the sea a hundred
Years ago when I was in my teens,
And years go by
I turned into a man,
My childhood trapped within the
    sand.
I crawled through life
On broken glass,
Through hell.
It seems I wakened
My desires
And woke one day wet with sweat
Of fear.
Wet with the sweat of fear
As now with you.

marc almond

HER
I'll reveal your mother,
Come to me:
I'll take you to the safety of the
  womb.

Tell me your secrets,
Sorrow, tears and darkness.

Pour out your heart,
Sorrow, tears and darkness.

You'll be a fool,
A fool for love.

And hell had never
Seemed so good
As when I lost my soul
Because a fool for love.

Help me, please to find my way.

HER
Look into the mirror of my eyes

Your kiss has clouded up my mind –

HER
And tell me what you see:

I was a fool, a fool for love.

HER
It's not your love I need.

I cried for those forsaken times,

HER
You'll see

She took my soul in Istanbul,
Sorrow tears and darkness,
She left me on that night to die.

HER
These are the pleasures
Beyond your dreams.

These are the pleasures beyond all
  my dreams.

I am lost –
Help me to find my way
Here in a world where
Angels fear to gaze.
My love is doomed to die
Alone tonight in Istanbul
And I a fool
For
Love.

death's diary

london 1989

On Monday I took a flower,
Dried it in my hand,
Covered it in poison,
And threw it on the land.
On wasted ground it tried to root
But choked upon the sand.

And there's room in my diary
For you, my friend,
And there's room in my diary for
    you.

On Tuesday I took a bird –
Such pain to hear it sing –
I blackened it with petrol
And oiled its little wings.
I tainted the breeze
As I threw it to the wind.

And there's room in my diary
For you, my friend,
And there's room in my diary for
    you.

On Wednesday I took a man.
He begged, 'please help me die',
For he lay in pain and suffering,
It made his loved ones cry.
I can be terrible and gentle
In the blinking of an eye.

And there's room in my diary
For you, my friend,
And there's room in my diary for
    you.

On Thursday I took a woman
Heavy with a child.
My old friend rape had paid a visit,
Stayed a little while.
In a back street I touched her
With a wire and a smile.

And there's room in my diary for
    you,
My friend,
And there's room in my diary for
    you.

On Friday I took a city,
Cursed it with a plague,
Powdered crystals, smoking pipes,
To crush and to enslave.
And a row of dirty needles
Lines the route onto the grave.

And there's room in my diary
For you, my friend,
And there's room in my diary
For you.

On Saturday I took a country
Praying for the rain,
Parched throats and swollen lips
Without a harvest grain.
And I wiped out generations,
And I'd do it all again.

And there's room in my diary
For you, my friend,
And there's room in my diary for
    you.

On Sunday I took the world,
A bomb I did employ –
Seven days to create life
And one day to destroy
Every woman, every man
Every girl and boy.

And there's room in my diary
For you, my friend,
And there's room in my diary for
    you.

Now as I close my diary
And I've made my final date,
I blow away the ashes
And I stoke the smoking grate.
I've no distinction between pain and
    joy,
No line twixt love and hate.

And there's room in my diary for
    you, my friend,
And there's room in my diary for
    you.

there is a bed

london 1985

There is a bed where I can end my days
To think about the road I've run,
The miles I've come.
There is a bed where troubles melt away,
My lonely hours or hours with you,
The times that we've come through.

There is a bed where we shared times of love
And out of love those nights are
Memories best forgot.
We argued about trivial things
And slept apart: a wall we built
Among the sheets.

There is a bed where sickness left its touch
And fever damped the sheets where
I would shake all night,
Cold burning on my brow,
Hallucinations here and now,
A fight to live or die.

There is a bed where first we both made love
And left the marks, reminders of how good it felt:
The hard, the soft, the sweat in midnight's hour,
We built the fort, we climbed the tower.

There is a bed where years will make us wise,
Truth and lies defeat, despise and forgiving,
The sheets our cradle birth to death,
The twists and turns of love, the life we're living.
There is a bed where nights I lay awake
To think about my future, to forget my past,
My bed a boat to sail the seas
To land where safety find me gripping to the mast.

And though I feel the years slip through my fingers,
Sorrow lingers and won't go away.
There is a bed that is my sanctuary,
A bed where I can end my days.

the gambler

On a dark night
In a lost hour
In a town built from
Neon and chrome,
Where Las Vegas
Eats the desert
In an old run-down casino

There the gambler
Slapped his money down,
Dirty dollars, one hundred or more,
Placed a last bet
On a poker game,
Crossed his heart for a winning score.
But the players at the table,
Two men of a phantom creed
Seemed to play with sombre purpose
And a reason other than pure greed.
And the gambler felt his back freeze
And fear brushed his aging brow
For he'd seen those men before in his dreams,
Here they sat before him now.
And the one
Smoothed back his black hair
With a comb slicked by Brylcreem and grease,
Flipped the cards with a flippancy
Of a wily and slippery ease.

With a sharp suit,
Shade of lilac,
On a shuffle he made the cards sing.
Gold studs and cigarettes,
Rubies set in a skull ring.

And the other,
Of the clergy,
With a collar and a robe of pale ivory,
Silver grey at the temples
And a smile that was stern and was kindly.

Jack of Hearts
Made way for aces,
Became faces, of family and friends
Until the deck showed him a picture
Of his life from beginning to end.

Here Reverend Life, he flipped an ace
And the gambler felt the blood in his heart –
For he knew this was the game of games
And it would need all the reverend's art

Anger, lust and gluttony:
The gambler's sins hit hard,
Each failure and each feature
Mapped out in the slippery cards.

Greasy Mr D flashed a winning grin
And stood facing Reverend Life;
The reverend paled as he saw the score
The gambler felt the pain as a knife.

His troubles, tribulations,
Revelations and regrets:
A wife, a child, a fight, a trial,
Turned by the hand of death.
And the gambler
Saw his hands stained
With the blood of his family ties,
And with the yellow smile of Mr D
In his mind, he crumples and dies.

And these great men from different worlds
Faced each other and shook of hand.
The reverend shrugged, 'Ah well, next time'
And departed for heavensland.

And the flames leapt,
And the souls screamed,
And the cards scattered round the room.
And life is always a gamble,
A game from the cradle to tomb.

your kisses burn

london 1988

for nico

HIM   You make a fire
Here in my heart;
Your kisses burn me
Sending sparks.
Auras fade,
Charisma pales,
Your kisses burn –
They scorch my soul.

And world without end,
Through tempest and storm,
Your kisses my fire –
Your love keeps me warm.

When your kisses burn,
Why are my lips like ice?

HER   I'll make a fire
There in your heart,
Made not of love
But only hate.
And for the fuel
Will be your soul,
An inferno
To consume you whole.

And world without end,
Through tempest and storm,

HIM   My soul be your fire.

HER   To keep my heart warm.
With my touch,
I'll freeze your heart.

marc almond

come in, sweet assassin

Come in,
Sweet assassin,
How will I ever know you love me
Unless you hurt me?
Put your head down on the pillow,
Take off your dancing shoes
And rest your gypsy feet.

Come in,
Sweet assassin,
You've got nothing to steal
And nothing to lose.
Just call in when you're passing,
I've forgotten how it feels
Not to trust someone.

Come in,
Sweet assassin,
And do just what you have to do.
Make it quick,
Don't fool around,
Ignore all sombre warnings
Not to succumb to love,
To keep my heart locked up
For ever more.

The rings upon your fingers
Boast of what you took from
    others,
What you're going to take from me.
The taint of perfume lingers
On the clothes of those
That fell into your arms.
You charm and move in for the kill.

eautiful twisted night   141

other words on other nights

old jack's charms

london 1989

It was in the tattoo parlour
Where he engraved their names,
Words a-winding round his
   shoulder,
Reminders now he's older.

In the magic of the parlour,
Down his arm unwinds a story:
Love and hate and Mum and Dad
In flames of hope and glory;

A mermaid and a schooner
Tells us he was once at sea;
A heart pierced by an arrow
Tells us once in love was he;
And a dragon spitting fire
He's forgotten what that's for,
But tattooed on his mind
Is a reminder of the war.

He gave up tattooing lovers
Where no room for any others:
A line through every sweetheart
With another etched below.
In every port a stormy girl –
They loved him and they loved him
   so.
Each one for all to see adorned
With cupids and with bows.

A mermaid and a schooner
Tells us he was once at sea;
A heart pierced by an arrow
Tells us once in love was he;
And a dragon spitting fire
He's forgotten what that's for,
But tattooed on his mind
Is a reminder of the war.

In the magic of the parlour,
Swapping laughter, swapping
   stories,
Where the words are often hard
And the air is always blue.
He remembers all his mates from
   then –
He lost a couple, maybe ten,
Their headstone on his forearm as a
   crucifix tattoo.

Now he leans upon the bar
With a mysterious air,
And the ladies gather round
To view his decorated arms.
He'll tell them of each scroll and
   line
And other scars not so fine,
And they always want to see
A little more of Old Jack's Charms.

pushin' ink
(for spring)

There is a story on his arm,
A secret on his chest,
A lover gone upon his thigh,
A threat upon his ass.
Detailed scrolls of winding ink
Like tendrils round a tree,
Declarations, observations,
Gleaming mysteries.
A wicked dagger, slim and sharp,
That pierces skull, and rose,
Deathly symbols,
Love's sweet signs:
A treasure map for one who knows.
A curl around a nipple,
A spear through a shoulder blade,
Two pulsing hearts, a diving swallow,
Anchors, ace of spades.
Needle-threaded reminders
Bravura crafted on the flesh,
A serpent in the crevices,
Writhing where it's wet.
Paintings for his lifetime,
Decorations for parade,
A carpet for the Devil,
Coloured from the shades
Of hell.
Vermilion slashes purple,
Bruised turquoise, indigos,
A plumage for a cockatoo:
Comfort for all self-adoring matelots.
He wears them like his medals:
They tell stories of his wars,
Evocative, provocative,
They forbid him heaven's doors:
And for this he may be thankful?
Halos would never suit him well,
For he follows a trail of blood and ink,
To join all his friends
In Hell.

jackal jackal
marrakesh 1983

I dived into the pool,
The cool, the blue from heat,
The sun breathes fire
On Marrakesh
To burn the busy street.
My brow the wet of fever,
My throat the dry of sand,
Through passageways to dead ends,
A gauntlet of the hands.

Jackal jackal
Rise of hackle
Row of tombstone teeth,
Take me to the labyrinth,
The palace of the thief.

The shaking of the bus,
The ragged boys a-chanting,
My temple pounds with sights and
    sounds:
The stamping and the dancing.

My body feels so dizzy
As cobra snakes unwind,
Dark hands dart to my pockets
For anything they'll find.
Oh let me lead you, take you, feed
    you,
To the hungry souk.
Monkey grins and cumin skins,
Eyes so wise
And smile so young.

Jackal jackal
Rise of hackle
Row of tombstone teeth,
Take me to the labyrinth,
The palace of the thief.

My face on the pavement,
The grit deep in my skin,
Arms around my shoulders,
The grazing of my skin.

And he watches the sun go up,
He watches the sun go down;
I dived into the pool,
I dived in deep to drown.

Jackal jackal
Row of tombstone teeth,
Take me to the labyrinth,
The palace of the thief.

photograph by Jamie McLoud

marc almond

the river
london 1985

And he dances every night
Framed in candles
And white white light,
All is revealed
When all is too bright.
You're such a pleasure,
A wonderful pain
Makes me want
To never love again.
But sorrow always comes
To those with fickle fame.

And the tears are gonna come,
The tears are gonna come …

We are consumed by corruption,
Old before our time,
Hurt by others' hunger,
Scarred by love and greed (how I
   need).
How cruel the birthday of 17 –
Youth behind you,
The long years ahead
Showing you what you might have
   been
Instead of drifting, drifting, drifting.

And the tears are gonna come,
The tears are gonna come …

Foundations crumble,
Walls subside,
We all break apart,
When there's heartache inside.
Hold back those years,
Those tears,
With a futile pride (we're gonna
   come clean).

Beware of love
And of dark-eyed men:
They're sweet and they're tender,
But they have no hearts –
Just long-smashed
Cruel shards of broken glass.

And the tears are gonna come,
The tears are gonna come …

And all those songs
That made me cry
Keep flooding back;
And years of new discovery and you
Disturbing my dreams,
Now we're flowing down that river,
Heading for the delta.
I don't know which way to flow
But my heart's a forest fire
And your's is a field of snow.

I don't know which way to flow.
I don't know which way
Don't know which way
To flow.

guiltless
1982

I have no need to hide my head in
    shame,
No need to shy from alternative
    games:
Guiltless.
Soft and sweet
Like a chocolate in the heat –
It drips and slides,
No longer hides
Itself.

Sex melts,
There are no holds,
Enjoying turning round the roles
And setting fire to the soul.
See it
And go for it –
Strike while the iron is hot,
Don't wait until the moment dies.
Take your pick
Because life is rich and full of it.
Go for it.

Shut my eyes
To loving lies
In the dark, in the dirt.
Have and hurt,
Have and hurt,
Like a biker in the summer heat.
Keep it sweet
Like a torn skin
On a shiny limb.
Rub it in
And go for it.

Take it to your wildest dream,
Take it to the extreme.
Take the rough
Forget the smooth
And choose
Locked encounters on the street.
The dirt, the hurt,
No more playing in a dark locked
    room,
No more lying about
Things life taught you to do.

See for it and go for it
Drink your fill
Guiltless
See it and go for it
In the dirt
Have and hurt
Keep it sweet
Rub it in
Go for it
Take it to the extreme
No need
The hurt
See it and go for it
Everytime you feel
To me joy
Go for it

Oh I bet your life
You're sick of the sight
Of those eat-in take-out throw-up
Pizza bars.
Love's just got to pass your way in
    time.
You smell of prison, smell of crime –
I just didn't want to say I told you so
Someone called,
'Hey, yesterday boy!
Take your well worn body away
    from my sight.'
Friends run like rats from a sinking
    ship
Leaving you naked to the night,
Now you're known as the last resort
By the vultures on the make.
They say,
'You have to eat the hamburger
To appreciate the steak.'

Chorus
You always feel the sting of words
As children are so cruel –
They called you ugly ugly head
When you were at school.
You've tried to make the best of
    things
But it seems you've given in.
They call you ugly ugly head,
Something makes you feel the living
    sin.

Things must feel so insecure
When you're on your last legs –
You're swimming in the coffee pot,
Drowning in the dregs.
But you haven't got the sense to die
(Or get a decent job),
To look into a mirror
Or at the very worst, some kind of
    God,
You need something to believe in –
I just wish it was yourself.
Try to summon up the gut to rectify
Your ailing health.

For there's something round the
    corner,
Waitin' just outta sight
That'll stop you feeling low and
    limp
And naked to the night.

You always feel the sting of words
As children are so cruel –
They called you ugly ugly head
When you were at school.
You've tried to make the best of
    things
But it seems you've given in.
They call you ugly ugly head,
Something makes you feel the living
    sin.

UGLY UGLY UGLY
UGLY UGLY UGLY
UGLY UGLY UGLY
UGLY HEAD!

kept boy

a duet written for agnes bernelle
london 1988

HER　　He brings me flowers every morning,
　　　　He brings the world into my bed,
　　　　He makes my bedroom into springtime:
　　　　Violets, gardenias, roses red.
　　　　He brings me tea and serves me chocolate
　　　　And I lick honey from his fingertips.
　　　　He makes the world a little brighter,
　　　　He makes my shadows a little lighter.

HIM　　I know where she keeps her money,
　　　　I know she has but little time,
　　　　I know she completely trusts me,
　　　　I've got her where I want her – she's completely mine.
　　　　I've seen her brooches thick with diamonds,
　　　　I've seen her count her beads of jet and pearl,
　　　　I'll bleed her of her gold and riches,
　　　　I'm so happy that oblivious the bitch is.

CHORUS　　Kept boy, you kept me enraptured,
　　　　Kept boy, you keep breaking my heart,
　　　　Kept boy, I kept you encaptured,
　　　　Kept boy, keep playing the part.

HER　　He cooks me dinner with the trimmings,
　　　　He polishes my silverware.
　　　　With tears of joy my eyes are brimming,
　　　　Without him my world would be very bare.

HIM　　I know where she keeps her papers –
　　　　Her testaments, her deeds to the house.
　　　　Her trusting look has me in stitches:
　　　　I'm so happy that oblivious the bitch is.

HER   He brings me flowers every morning,
He brings the papers to my bed,
Opens the curtains to my bedroom
And chases bad dreams from my head.

HIM   And as we celebrate your birthday –

HER   The one you thought would be my last –

HIM   There's something bitter in the champagne –

HER   Something working very fast.

HIM   Oh, how I'm feeling very dizzy,
The ceiling, the ceilings are becoming roundabouts.

HER   I caught your eyes upon my riches:
Not so oblivious this bitch is.

CHORUS

HER   Kept boy, you kept me enraptured,
Kept boy, no more playing the part,
Kept boy, I'll keep you forever and ever and ever,
Kept boy, forever and ever, and ever.

beautiful twisted night

suicide saloon

written for agnes bernelle
london 1996

In a futuristic city,
At the Suicide Saloon,
I danced with a dead man
To my favourite funeral tune.
In a blur of broken neon
I danced among the fruit machines,
On the dance floor of destruction
Among the broken dreams.
I tangoed with the dead-eyed
Of the cold concrete estate
And bossanova'd over
A death that's worse than fate.
I danced in red-light corners
With the children selling souls
And with the ladies of the lamplight
I danced some rock 'n' roll.

We didn't have a future,
We couldn't see the moon,
In the back room
Of the Suicide Saloon.

In a futuristic city,
At the Suicide Saloon,
We let go with some techno
To illuminate the gloom.
We swished under the fairy lights
In a mirror-ball malaise
With a door whore
And a troubadour
Who'd both seen better days.
I raised my glass
And did exotic dances on the bar
With a tabloid reporter
And a ruined superstar.
I mamboed with the housewives
Desperate for a thrill
And rhumba'd with their husbands
They were desperate to kill.

We didn't have a future,
We couldn't see the moon,
In the back room
Of the Suicide Saloon.

Before we all go down
In a sea of hopelessness
Let's go and get the priest
And get him to confess.
There never was a Jesus,
There never was a God,
Because the priest is in here (with us
    sinners) –
Now don't you think that's odd?

marc almond

In a futuristic city,
At the Suicide Saloon,
I hustled with a hustler
Working the room.
The floor show was a stripper
Who was way past her prime,
The bar man was a leather boy
In pan stick five and nine.
The doorman was a squealer,
The manager a fag,
The dj was a dealer,
Selling downers to dykes in drag.
I was having such a riot
Admiring all this art
I didn't see the world
Falling apart.

We didn't have a future
Because we couldn't see the moon
In the back room
Of the Suicide Saloon.

Come on and dance –
Who cares if bombs are falling,
Isn't that eternity calling?

Just dance.

song of sighs (come the morning)
london 1989

If I searched for the saddest song in
    the world
I'd find it in your sighs,
As I sleep each night in your loving
    arms
Dreaming of an ocean wide.
Your folded wings made of golden
    down,
On your brow the lines of time,
For I think just like a little boy,
With a little boy's mind.

You came to me upon the storm
Far across the ocean wide,
You braved the troubled dreams I
    dreamed
To embrace me like the tide;
To calm my heart, to soothe my
    soul,
To make me worldly wise,
For I looked at life like a little boy,
With a little boy's eyes.

You flew into my arms
On golden wings,
Your love goes on forever like the
    sea
And in your loving arms
The tide is turning
And I will be a young man come the
    morning.

You showed to me the sins of man,
Both sides of the ocean wide;
The troubles of the world,
The sorrow that we hide inside.
Please stay with me forever –
We must never stray apart
For I felt love like a little boy,
With a little boy's heart.

When comes the time to fly away
Back across the ocean wide
You will leave me with a memory
Of a little boy's pride.
With the North Star as your
    compass,
Sail away on golden wings –
But I know that wings that take
    away
Can also bring.

If I searched for the saddest song in
    the world
I'd find it in your sighs,
For I look at life like a young man
    now,
With a young man's eyes.

marc almond

the end of new york

1997

There's a funeral for the bright
    young things,
Buried as a diva sings
A final hymn to glitter
While our tears fall flat.
Like yesterday's champagne
Cold winds down Eighth Avenue –
The pleasure palaces we knew
Are boarded up.
We'll never see their stained velvet
    delights again –
The 'David', 'The Adonis Lounge',
'The Show Palace' have closed
    down
Where do the lovers of the dark go
    now?
All the dance beats fade
And the notices are served,
I'll always remember that last song I
    heard
At the end of New York,
At the end of New York.

The end of New York came on a
    day
That was as grey as the hair
On the mayor of New York.
He turned off the speakers,
Turned up the lights
And the corners shone white
For a better quality of life.
And the night didn't fall anymore,
Closed was a word on each door.

No more dancing,
No more drinking,
And nobody calling for more.
Only tears for the hustler,
The stripper, the whore.
And funeral purple
And black to mourn
Was the coat that I wore
At the end of New York,
The end of New York.

Annointed in neon,
We sing in dark themes
For a city that caters
For all of our dreams.
The song of the diva
Is sung low and sad,
Echoes down the glass canyons
For good times we had.
She dabs at her tears
And beckons a cab,
Stands in the rain
And holds out her hand.
But one never comes –
They're all taking the tourists
To Disneyland
On Forty-second Street.
Whoever planned it?

The end of New York,
The end of New York,
And there, at a mirror
The skeletal mayor,
Applying red lipstick
And gold nylon hair,
Smiles a chill smile,
A deathly grimace
For the place they called New York.

show palaces

the show palace
new york 1993

where do the lovely lovers of the dark go now, the worshippers in the temple of flesh, the shadow people – now the show
palace has closed down, the david, the adonis lounge?

23.00 THE SHOW PALACE, EIGHTH AVE, NEW YORK
a room shadowy in the muted red light, occasionally a reflec-
tion caught in the mirror tiles, a muffed distorted disco tape
and unintelligible announcement tells us to appreciate carlos
or jesus (where else would you find jesus but in a temple?).
jesus is sexy. jesus and the gods of flesh. the room is heavy
with sex scent and musky dark sweat and scented lube oil the
effect is heady, surreal and serious. four of the five enormous
black and latino guys dance lazily and zombie-like in a semi-
state of crack trance on the small strewn stage rubbing oil
into their lithe bodies and stretching their large semi-erect
and oiled penises into forever, like a snake dance in the temple to the great god erotica. occasionally they leave the stage
and straddle members of the audience drawing out dollars
from the spectators' pockets with their magical hustler powers – money stuffed into socks and boots for one more minute
of close attention. in the dark recesses and deep corners they
linger for longer, straddling and thrusting, larger amounts of
money getting more exotic attentions.

24.00 THE GAIETY THEATRE, TIMES SQUARE, NEW YORK
it's the final show of the day, the air is twice as thick with dare,
anticipation and sex. fourteen boys of mostly straight origin
and toned white-american apple-pie stock take turns to perform and sell their wares to an audience of mostly older gentlemen. against a cheap sparkling curtain of the purest

marc almond

tantalising glamour, they dance, crouch, spin and flex to classic and current disco and house tunes. beautifully fleshed and marbled, perfect looking bodies, bruise- and needle-mark free, thrust- and pose-defining buttocks and pecs, living pages from the athletic model guild. sweet homeboy faces, freckles, eager-puppy eyes, hustler grins, sometimes a tuft or two of hair in all the right places, sometimes near-shaped and teen-like backward baseball caps, white socks and short fuck-me cowboy boots for the tips and added sleaze 'erotic erotic put your hands all over my body' moans a familiar diva as eyes meet eyes and dollar touches torso. after removing their few clothes, plain shirt/black jeans, they strut their stuff before leaving the stage for a few moments. one imagines backstage a quick bump of coke, a girlfriend doing her stuff and limp members jolt into brief action. they return stiffly, perky, proud, and erect; some aren't successful in rising to the occasion, nerves, too much coke, too much business, but most meet the demand. they take a bow to the enthusiastic applause and seats clatter as they hurriedly empty as gentlemen beat a nasty path to the side-stage lounge to negotiate with the young dancer and a booming distorted voice bids us to put our hands together for the very talented joey. later back at the dancer's hotel, maybe the president hotel, off times square, a further performance, more private, maybe a little more awkward, takes place, cost approximately $200 – don't suck, get sucked or only fuck. if it's the last show, maybe come, only maybe. girlfriend? back home in connecticut 'yeah she knows.'

amsterdam

1989 20.00 it's raining and cold in amsterdam and there is a mist from the canals that gets on your chest and up your nose, making you sniff and wheeze, chilling you through. what do you do but look for warmth as you walk the street at night? i walked through the narrow streets one night and stopped to look into the little windows with lace curtains. windows lit in red, in ultra-violet purple and crimson pink, at girls of all shapes and sizes, beautiful, beckoning, warm and inviting. in one such window a black amazon goddess is sitting on a stool chewing on a chicken leg. grease ran down her chin and i thought of one of those biblical epics where whores of sodom always seemed to be tearing at chicken legs. she beckoned me in with her greasy fingers, her nails pearl white in the ultraviolet light. she was wearing a black leotard, her huge breasts falling out at either side, huge gold-hoop earrings and painted pink lips (the lipstick paint messed up from the chicken grease). she is from exotic africa, she looks like a sorceress but there is something of whoopi goldberg about her. perhaps it's her hair woven into hundreds of fine braids of ribbon gold. i open the door and pop my head in, immediately i am hit by the scent of a deliciously sleazy cheap perfume and a scarletness that emanates from the regulation brothel flock.'come in, come in.' she pulls me into her lair, quoting the price in gilders, and my mental arithmetic quickly works it out in english. twenty-five quid. a goddess for twenty-five quid – what a bargain. suddenly all is warm and the cold air of amsterdam is gone.

21.00 we visit the grapevine, a transsexual drag whorehouse. the girls are all beautiful and angular. they linger around the bar and in the half-lit corners, veiled in shadow, eyes narrow and glittering, like panthers waiting to pounce. elegant, cigarettes drip from slim fingers that sparkle with rings ending in purple and red two-inch talons. madam sherry informs the clientele: 'this is a whorehouse where men can wear women's clothes and if you don't like it, fuck off.'

there is a stage above the bar for cabaret performers and we watch the beautiful androgynous zette perform a song (i think it's called 'creatures of the night') in the tallest spike heels and black leotard. this is the second time this week we have seen zette. the other day at the anvil in manhattan's meat district we saw him perform a lipsync mime to 'youth' and 'bedsitter'.

a night drive through beirut
1994

23.00 in a city with no speed limits, no traffic lights and no order, a night drive through bombed-out beirut – a city decimated by seventeen years of war – is a terrifying and thrilling experience. our driver, one of the wealthier inhabitants of this shelled city of two worlds – simply, the very wealthy and the very poor – knows all its secrets, its nooks and crannies. there is another world: a third world, the gay night world. from fenced-off sites, dark skeletal buildings, block upon block of blackened soot and brick, are haunted by families still living among the ruins, buildings sliced in half, shell-shattered and pock-marked with bullet holes – onwards we drive through dark winding streets, past apartment buildings where men were once chained to radiators for years, to the neon of new nightclubs springing up among the rubble for this beaten up city – once the glittering riviera of the middle east, it is now dusting off its jewellery and trying to come back to life.

our bmw driver takes me to a darkened backstreet where the road is mud, cars drive round and round circling, stopping, looking, signalling, driving round the block and circling again like predators in a mating game: recognising, eyeing up and stopping to sniff before moving in for the kill or making off to find another. these car cruisers go round and round for hours before making a decision and finally pairing off to go home. there are about ten cars playing this furtive game – our driver tells us that this ritual is played out every night. beirut, i am told, is the gayest place in the middle east. our driver enters into the courtship ritual, eyeing up the male drivers, pausing and dismissing and making dates for later. he tears off on the main road at over 90mph, past billboards and lit façades. this city is full of such secrets and half truths, trying to appear normal while behind the scenes everything is falling apart. earlier in our hotel – the best in beirut i am told – while eating dinner in the restaurant, i watched the waiters chase a rat around the room and club it to death next to my table – its mushed body taken away on a shovel. everything is not quite as it seems.

back in the car our next stop is a gay massage parlour. up the stone steps into a small stone house, a hovel with no windows, a flagstone floor, low ceiling and a smallest pretence of being a gymnasium – dumb-bells, weights, a minor piece of rusted gym equipment. a smiling muscle man waits behind a counter.

i am taken to a small room where a younger man, without speaking a work of english, signals for me to remove my clothes. there is a massage table, and a bucket of warm water, cockroaches run freely. the man smiles and points at the table. he removes his clothes until he stands naked, muscles oiled and gleaming. he pours warm water over me – it's refreshing in the sticky heat and he gives me a relaxing massage. i gather that if i want extra then i have to make the first move, but i imagine that sex involves no reciprocation and the masseur is the only active participant – i decide to just enjoy the warm water massage.

after paying the man at the counter, we take off again in the car, tearing through the night to another destination. this time it's the promenade area of beirut known as the corniche. the sea front is busy with activity, all male. our driver informs me that you can have anyone you want, just ask, it's as simple as that. lines of cars are parked along the front, as young men chat to other young men, some flirting and camping around –

others just looked solid, asserting their position of masculinity in such posing and preening – the atmosphere is happy, unthreatening, little groups chatting, idling, gossiping – like any group of gay boys would anywhere else in the world. younger boys of heartbreaking beauty wait hopefully, available for a small price and all with love in their eyes.

six months later back at home in london i watched the news on television: israeli helicopters swooped down on beirut, firing missiles indiscriminately, and i recognised the corniche area, devastated and smoking. the same place where all the young gay men had relaxed freely, so happily, and i thought of their faces and their optimism, and i wondered if any of them had been there when the guns struck.

terance sellers' torture chamber

2.00 terance (alias angel stern) is new york's most famous dominatrix and author of a book, *the correct sadist*. aloof, beautiful, flame haired and dressed in black, she invites us to view her house of torture and to meet the ladies who work there. inside the elegant house behind unassuming doors is her secret world – decorated minimally, rooms stylishly painted in black and grey and red. there is a huge rack, a four-poster bed on which to shackle clients, some stocks, and, laid out like surgical instruments, twigs, canes and rods for the businessman's pleasure. mistress stern opens a wardrobe in which hang various outfits and uniforms. among the regulation fantasy wear nestles a little frilly pink dress to fit a young girl of nine or ten. 'this is our most popular fantasy outfit', mistress stern tells us. 'the businessmen just love to try and squeeze themselves into it.'

the baghdad club
1987

the baghdad club is a live porno sex club in the heart of the red light *barriochino* area in barcelona. down the winding streets smelling of sewers, past the little cabaret theatres showing bizarre drag shows billed as 'family entertainment'. onward past prostitutes, the roughest and oldest in barcelona sit in the street on wooden chairs, fanning themselves and clutching their cardigans around their huge motherly breasts. onward until you come to a sign that says 'baghdad porno show'. entrance fee is about thirty pounds, down stairs that lead to an arabic-style temple interior with little columns covered in mirrored tiles. on a small stage, veiled in red is a revolving podium on which the acts rotate to display every angle for the audience's advantage. a disembodied booming voice, overly reverbed, announces the acts as the lights dim.

an exuberant blonde in a cowboy hat bounces bare-breasted around the stage making jokes in spanish about penis sizes (indicating small or large with her fingers) as she

points at hapless members of the audience. the climax of her act takes place on a mechanical rodeo horse that is placed on the stage. from the saddle a large plastic dildo protrudes. she rides the horse and the dildo, shouting wildly and waving her cowboy hat in the air. the second act is a comedian in a sequined jacket who tells risqué and just plain crude

marc almond

jokes in spanish. his gestures indicate the jokes are largely about breasts, penises, sex – and, from the reaction of the audience, they appear to be quite amusing.

next are two post-op transsexuals who perform amid a large spider's web constructed from chains stretched across the stage. one pretends to be the fly, the other takes the role of the spider. they clamber towards each other; the spider is endowed with a dildo and an intention to use it on the fly. when the spider eventually catches the fly in an embrace, a strange sex act ensues to a specially recorded sexy synthesiser soundtrack that fills the small theatre with an eerie discordance. as the transsexuals hang upside down we can see the jagged scars on the underside of their breasts, the results of the cheap operations. finally they take their bow and leave the stage. their place is immediately taken by a standard magician who performs a series of well known card tricks involving rabbits from hats, scarves from sleeves and bouquets of feathers and flowers.

next to come, so to speak, is a black and white act. an african black man and a large-breasted white with frozen faces woman go through a series of sexual motions. as they lie emotionless on the revolving podium the man is coaxed into hardness by his partner as she whispers professional sweet secrets into his ear. on a previous visit to the baghdad i recall this section of the show was similar, still involving a white woman but with a dwarf instead of the black man. after the ejaculation (achieved without facial expression) they take a bow, semen still dripping from the end of his penis, and it's time for the finale.

two women take the stage, both obviously transsexuals in a

state of change. one of them is a tall blonde, the other even taller, an amazon about 6 feet 5 inches (reminiscent of a drag jayne mansfield) – she stands on the revolving podium looking in a hand mirror dressed in a red chiffon baby-doll nightdress. the two of them start to kiss, to caress and undress, gradually falling to their knees. the blonde amazon, who looks entirely plastic, removes her nightdress, stands and removes her g-string to reveal a still-intact penis. the other transsexual begins to suck and caress the penis until, after much labour, it gradually becomes erect. they then lie down on the podium (still revolving) and the smaller one mounts the amazon to the cue of the synthesised sex music and flashing lights.

chi chi la rue's night at the eros

eighth avenue, new york 1996

20.00. the eros is the only male palace of porn left on eighth avenue, the rest were swallowed up by the great god disney. it's a plucky little cinema, its brave blue neon eros sign a beacon to lovers of male erotic dancing and blurred celluloid encounters of male-on-male flesh. the eros sign, in 1950s fashion, promises something camp and kitsch and almost cheesecake. i think of the photos in physique magazines from the 1950s and 1960s – men dressed as gladiators, men spreadeagled on tiger-skin rugs, men with oily quiffs, men with sculpted muscles and fixed dimpled grins with eyes full of fun against glitter backdrops, men in posing pouches with anchor tattoos, biker boys in leopard skin tussling each other like playful puppies on heat, sexy and innocent. the word 'eros' in blue neon makes me dream of these things – it makes me dream of bobby kendal in *pink narcissus* – that strange erotic movie from a lost decade by follies de hommes.

dreaming once in this way i entered through the turnstile into the murky recesses of the eros, and was bought to my senses by out-of-focus hardcore images and muffled grunts of pleasure, or pain. the seats, once salacious red velvet, were now dulled, faded and broken, inhabited by silent sheepish figures, some hand in motion, some asleep, all somebody's husband. hands grabbed at me and i realised i was being hustled and propositioned by two or three latin boys in matching briefs and bruises, red and purple, and stained with baby oil. they wanted to take me downstairs to a place probably even darker and murkier, past a broken toilet to a dressing room. they wanted dollars, and far too many dollars because these weren't the little latin cat-boy extras from a madonna video – these were hustler trash that even the show palace rejected.

one of them checked his watch and said to his friend 'one more dance and then i'm going to the video booths.'

(the video booths, if you're wondering, are beneath the show palace, in the basement of a sex shop, a line of male video booths showing pornographic movies, outside the booths, waiting, a line of black and latin hustlers. hustlers circle the customers and the crack dealers circle the hustlers. the monitor dishing out tokens for booths is paid a couple of dollars to turn a blind eye, 'keep it moving guys, get in them booths now', he keeps shouting and the procession keeps shuffling. customer and hustler would disappear into a booth and five minutes later the hustler would emerge and slope around a corner to buy some coke or crack. this went on all night and all day and got packed around 18.00 in the evening when business around times square finished.)

the film suddenly stops mid-orgasm, the lights dim and the boys half-heartedly gyrate to some muffled disco music, taking only a small pause before fleecing the audience of any loose change. but that was then. the eros has now had something of a revamp, a coat of paint, a dash of sparkle. the 1950s-style eros sign looks braver and bluer than ever and shouts down decimated eighth avenue, 'i'm still here'. outside a sign proclaims 'tonight – chi chi la rue'. porn director, performer, personality and all-round priestess of porn has brought glamour and tease back to the eros, and as i enter the theatre i am dazzled by a mirror ball and blinded by the sequins on chi chi's frock as she paces back and forth, light exploding christmas all over the stage. burlesque is back as chi chi brandishes porno magazines (featuring her celluloid stud muffins), turns the air blue with cracks, jokes and the cheapest asides of the filthiest tints. she introduces a selection of porno princes to tease us and delight our jaded palates. the stage resembles a pierre et gilles set with shades of pink and twinkling fairy lights (well, not quite pierre et gilles, but those cheaper imitations who aspire to be them) and it feels good to be sleazy again.

chi chi calls us all naughty boys and slaps us with porno mags and we quake in our seats as this thundering sequined dynamo storms up and down the aisles. the porno playmates form a fetching tableau while a misplaced attendant, standing self consciously at the edge of the fraying lurex curtain, eyes us all suspiciously for signs of over excitement. we dare not be too excited or chi chi will come at us, her boobs like sequinned battleships, and slap us over our heads with a shiny unthumbed copy of inches. yes, i can dream of bike boys in togas, posing-pouched centurians, discus-throwing tony curtis lookalikes and sailors on fur rugs and almost, for a moment … almost, feel innocent again.

the reeperbahn
hamburg, germany 1986

23.00 lurid signs enticing with promise beckon you down to what appears to be an underground car park. the place is pink, purple and red with fluorescent and neon illuminating the entire space with a hot, intoxicating sexual glow. against the random concrete pillars are beautiful painted half-dressed women in white leotards, exposing leg, thigh and cleavage. they all have charlie's angels hair, all farrah-fawcett flicks. the make-up is a little thickly applied and the occasional bead of perspiration breaks out above their red and pearl-pink lips – lips now mouthing and forming the letter 'o', lips being sucked in and licked and long painted nails beckoning. fingers stretching and curling, eyes narrowing. words with a german tang, but an unmistakable meaning, words that sound almost the same in any language. the light, the heat, cheap perfume, melting make-up, hair spray, fresh perspiration make your head full with sexual thoughts, confusion and a dangerous thrill. words crisscross in your ear and hands pull you and stroke you, guide you to them, pull you to them. you are captured in the confusion. eventually one of these sirens snares you and you are hers. she speaks of good times, different types of good times for different amounts of money. you find yourself saying 'yes, yes, yes' to anything, anything!

now it is too late because suddenly you find yourself being taken up a back stairway to a sparse but warm and comfortable room. it looks clean but it has hosted this scene a thousand times before. deutchmarks are spirited out of your pocket by those slender fingers with the purple nails. she disappears and you are left alone for what seems like twenty

marc almond

minutes. thoughts of lust are replaced by thoughts of confusion, then deflation, then disappointment. just as angers pops up in your head she reappears with condoms. she rolls one on you then two too her head begins to dance. 'you said mouth fuck?' 'no', you say 'i want the full action.'

'ahh – when i say "fuck" i mean mouth fuck, if you want pussy fuck then that's more deutchmarks', she says, her head longer dancing. as you fall limp to rustle in your pocket for more money she applies more lipstick. you pay her. 'back in one moment' she says and disappears for twenty more minutes. she reappears and seems to sparkle a little more this time 'now we can begin', she says. sex now the last thing on your mind, you shut your eyes and try to rise to the occasion. she is skilled in bringing these matters to a close quickly. soon you are back on the street, bathed in the lurid lights of the reeperbahn, a little flushed, a little relieved and a little empty of pocket.

the savoy
new york 1994

midnight. it's friday night and it must be buddha's big dick contest at the savoy bar, situated by the port authority bus terminal. the bar is stuffed to capacity with banjee boys and their girlfriends, young black and latin hustlers, a couple of transvestites taking a break from sally's hideaway (a sister transvestite bar up the street), dealers, dopers and strays, village queens out for a dash of low-rent sleaze and tattooed white boys out for the thrill. buddha, a fat toothless black man with grey curly hair, a diamanté earring and a long gold mandarin's fingernail is at one end of the bar. he is with a coterie of underage banjee boys he has promised the world, or the half world that he inhabits after dark. some wear the blue and yellow beads of the latin kings – i have made friends with members of the latin kings new york gang so my safety is assured in the bar and the street out front, which can get quite scary on forty-ninth street and ninth avenue. the gang members stand guard at the door with ever-watchful eyes. the girls, their hair in bangs and plaits hang dopily around their hustler boyfriends who ignore them – playing pool, passing joints and snorting coke in the bathroom. their woollen hats pulled down over their ears (giving them a cute goofiness), their teeth encased in gold, their pants hanging off their hips (one leg rolled up), their necks ringed with gold chains. they swagger around the pool table, shoulders slung low, hands curved inwards. at 1.30 buddha takes the stage and welcomes the crowd on a microphone with too much reverb. he berates the transvestites and dares anyone to enter the contest for the $50 prize – the crack dealers wait. there are two contestants tonight, they are waiting in the beer-storage room being blown by their girlfriends, trying by whatever

marc almond

means to get some life into their flaccid members (suffering from the effects of too much coke). the first to take the stage is a tall gangly black guy in a woollen hat. he provides a half-hard monster – the crowd yells its approval. buddha produces his ruler and measures the snake-like appendage. 'ten inches', shouts buddha and bends to kiss the snake with a gummy mouth. the sheepish contestant, looking a little peaky and sweaty, as his last pipe wore off some hours ago, slopes off into the back room to work up another inch and so his place is taken by rico, a latin boy with half his teeth missing. he runs out, quickly followed by his girl, before his proud erection flops and it's obvious he is not going to mea-sure up – nevertheless the crowd cheer him on. 'nine inches', proclaims buddha.

the crowd surges nearer to the stage in wonderment and awe, as if they have never seen such meat before.

rico runs off pulling his girlfriend with him to work a little hard. the first contestant, the gangly black guy runs up again, nearly falling over his own trousers which are round his ankles. grasping his piece, he has raised another half an inch. it's official. 'ten and a half inches', declares buddha, and the crowd is almost at frenzy point. buddha once more gums the guy's extra limb, causing acute humiliation, though of course the contestants can't complain – this is buddha's place and buddha's show, and beside he needs that pipe.

suddenly there is commotion as the door swings open. a tall mulatto boy with a huge mouth and a shock of curly hair strides in wearing an overcoat. pushing through the crowd he makes his way to the little platform. 'it's big bird', gasps one of the transvestites.

silence.

'he's gonna win it again', another shouts resignedly, and sure enough when big bird opens his overcoat he reveals the clear winner by a couple of inches.

'you bitches, i'm the biggest and the prettiest and it tastes good too', drawls the effeminate big bird, and he claims his $50 prize, much to the chagrin of the gangly black guy who has to make do with second place ($20) he's not disappointed for long though because the village queens are soon in discussion with him about making a donation of their own. the crowd disperses, boys leave with their girls, some with older gentlemen, and down on ninth avenue the crack dealer is waiting. some of the boys will take their elderly friends to the elk hotel round the corner on forty-second street for a short stay.

it is now a year later and buddha is no longer at the savoy. he was fired for letting too many of the latin kings into the bar to do drug deals. some say he's managing a bar downtown. the owners have moved in plastic tables with umbrellas which look truly surreal in the dark pokey little bar, and have removed the pool table. needless to say the place is empty. no more big dick show on a friday night either – never mind, i'm sure they'll soon see sense.